Who is right about God?

Who is right about God?

Thinking through
Christian attitudes
in a world of many faiths

Duncan Raynor

BOOKS

Winchester, U.K.
New York, U.S.A.

First published by O-Books, 2008
Reprinted, 2017
O-Books is an imprint of John Hunt Publishing Ltd., Laurel House, Station Approach,
Alresford, Hants, SO24 9JH, UK
office1@jhpbooks.net
www.johnhuntpublishing.com

For distributor details and how to order please visit the 'Ordering' section on our website.

A CIP catalogue record for this book is available from the British Library.

Printed and bound by CPI Group (UK) Ltd, Croydon, CR0 4YY, UK

We operate a distinctive and ethical publishing philosophy in all
areas of our business, from our global network of authors to
production and worldwide distribution.

This book is dedicated
in gratitude
and with love
to my dear wife
Caroline Ruth,
who has always encouraged me
to think clearly,
to speak honestly,
and to face up to issues
which need confronting.

Contents

Acknowledgements

As any student knows, reading what other people have written can be quite fun. Criticising it can be even more fun, and developing and discussing your own ideas can be the best fun of all. But writing down your ideas – that is far less fun. That is hard graft; it involves time and effort, and usually a few missed deadlines and more than a little midnight oil. That is why I have spent thirty years reading and teaching and discussing the ideas that are built up in this book, but only now have I got around to writing it. Even now it would not have happened without the generosity of my employers, the Foundation of the Schools of King Edward the Sixth in Birmingham, who gave me half a term's sabbatical from teaching, and the tolerance of my family, who saw domestic jobs left unfinished or even unstarted while I sat at the computer surrounded by books and notes. So my thanks to them.

There are so many others to whom thanks are owed that I cannot possibly mention all of them, but I do wish to mention some of the key players at King Edward's School in Birmingham, where I have had the privilege of teaching since 1994, and where the atmosphere of respect, critical thinking, and intelligent debate among both staff and students has done much to aid the development of my ideas. Colleagues of widely differing persuasions and beliefs have been supportive and encouraging, as well as rigorous and searching in their criticism. Among them, I have enjoyed the backing in this enterprise of two very different Chief Masters, Roger Dancey and John Claughton, and the stimulus of working alongside my specialist colleagues Anne Ostrowicz and Gill Hudson. In the wider Common Room I have benefited especially from discussions at various times with (in no particular order!) Tim Mason, Jeff Hancock, George Andronov, Stan Lampard, Stan Owen, Michael Daniel, John Cumberland, David Ash, Carol Southworth, and Jonathan Smith. I owe a particular debt to Howard Smith and Beccy Leaver, who kept my feet on the ground with their trenchant views on religion, and persisted in referring to this work as my 'pamphlet'. I hope they feel it has now outgrown that description. My ideas have also had to cope with the formidable intellectual firepower of my wife and children, Caroline, Becky, and Ben, all arts graduates with remarkable skill in the detection and exposure of specious argument. To all the above I offer my grateful thanks; but above all I must thank the generations of students on whom I have tried out these ideas and many more. We have enjoyed our discussions over the years, I think, and they have gone on into universities and beyond with an attitude of mind which values open and frank discussion of different ideas about God, truth, and religion. They may not agree with the position I adopt or the arguments I offer; but at least they agree that this is important stuff. I hope the reader will end up agreeing with that, too.

My final thanks are for veteran British folk fiddler Dave Swarbrick, who not only gave me permission to use the lyrics of his song 'Rosie', but graciously said he was 'delighted to see it put to such good use'. Nice support, that. It looks like the forces of good might be winning. I hope this book carries the fight a bit further.

DHR

Rosie

I know, Rosie, you're living in a world you didn't make;
And I know it's hard feeling happy,
when the things you want aren't even there to take.

Come on, Rosie, and rosin up the bow,
For the more I learn, it's the less I seem to know;
Lie down cozy, and let's learn to take things slow,
For the more I learn, it's the less I seem to know.

Throw away your uniform, now's the time to take life by the hand
Come on in and take your coat off,
Settle down and listen to the band.

Come on, Rosie, and rosin up the bow,
For the more I learn, it's the less I seem to know;
Lie down cozy, and let's learn to take things slow,
For the more I learn, it's the less I seem to know.

Dave Swarbrick

This is a fine song. If you want to listen to it, see the reading list for
CDs. If you want to know how it is relevant, you'll have to read all
the way to chapter 9.

1

So what's this all about?

On a shelf above my desk sits a carved wooden figure, about nine inches high. It portrays an elderly man, recognizably Chinese, sitting in a chair, dressed in traditional Chinese robes. I don't know how old it is, but I do know when and how it came into my family. A hand-written label on the back tells me that it was "given to Rev Grainger Hargreaves about 1886 by last member of family to become Christian".

Rev Grainger Hargreaves was a Wesleyan missionary in China, and he was also my great-grandfather. The figure is one of the few remaining artifacts which he and his wife brought back to this country when they returned home from what they called "the mission field". The statue is a testimony to the success of their missionary work. It is in fact an ancestor-figure, taken from a traditional Chinese ancestor-shrine, and it was handed over to the missionaries by a convert, presumably when the redundant family shrine was dismantled. This would have been a sign of the seriousness of the family's commitment to its new Christian faith. Despite its value to the family, and the respect and reverence due to ancestors in traditional Chinese culture, the shrine could not of course be kept after the family's conversion to Christianity. The new faith would not permit the veneration of idols. I can find the text in my great-grandfather's own Bible, presented to him on his commissioning as a missionary at Small Heath in Birmingham in 1878: "Thou shalt not make ... any graven image, or any likeness of any thing that is in heaven above, or that is in the earth beneath, or that is in the water under the earth: Thou shalt not bow down to them nor serve them, for I the Lord thy God am a jealous God." (Exodus 20.4–5). No doubt this was impressed upon the converts, and my little Chinese figure – perhaps the most important one, or maybe the oldest one, in the shrine – was presented to the missionary as a sign of good faith, and also as a sign that there was no going back. The decision was final, and the convert was saved from error and brought to the true faith. Provided he remained faithful, he was saved from damnation and hell fire, and brought into the community of salvation. Curiously, the little ancestor figure became a treasured artifact in another and very different family, and took on a new significance. Now he was a visible sign of success in missionary work.

And indeed my great-grandparents were successful. The records of the Wesleyan Missionary Society show that the North River Mission flourished. Many years later, in Oxford in the 1940s, my great-grandmother was still receiving letters from Canton with news of the mission and of the children and grandchildren of "her" converts.

My mother took great pleasure in her own old age in telling me about the family history and passing on a few letters and books from those days. She passed on some of the attitudes, too, as mothers tend to do. I was encouraged to be proud of this heritage, and as a teenager I was encouraged to attend a weekly Bible class, where I lapped up an evangelical, mission-oriented view of the Christian faith. I was taught – just as my great-grandfather had been in his day – that I must bear witness to my faith, that I must evangelize, that I must spread the truth. I was not quite taught that the unconverted would burn in hell-fire, but I was certainly left in no doubt that their fate would be much less desirable than the eternal bliss that awaited the Christian.

As a teenager, with all a teenager's uncritical enthusiasm, I took all this on board, and it was part of the cargo I carried forward towards university and ordination training in due course. When I thought to ask about the position of people who belonged to other religions, I received one of two answers. One was hard-line and uncompromising: they were in error, and they were damned unless they came to recognize the truth. So of course I must help them recognize the truth and never miss an opportunity to witness to them. The other answer was rather less judgmental: it was up to God what he decided about sincere believers in other faiths, but it had been revealed to us that Christianity was the true faith, and so I must help them recognize the truth and never miss an opportunity to witness to them. The practical upshot, you will have noticed, was the same in each case, but even then it was the second view that appealed to me more. I didn't think much more about it at that stage, though. It was easy not to, as a sheltered teenager in what was then a fairly prosperous white city district, and at a school and university in which religion was equated with Christianity and the religious life centered upon the chapel. Of course I could not fail to be aware, in a general sense, of the existence of people of other faiths in Britain, and in Birmingham, and even at Oxford University; but at that stage my experience was limited, and it was easy to remain at a distance from any serious engagement. I remained indifferent to them, moving as I did in a Christian setting, and moreover a pretty much white and Anglo-Saxon one. Many of us did, in those days.

So I entered my twenties, and not long after that my training for ordained service in the Church, as a rather sheltered idealist. I was aware in a general sort of way that there were questions to be asked about the relationship of Christianity with other faiths, but I was pretty content with the traditional answers. Essentially I was still living in my great-grandfather's world, where "The heathen in his blindness bows down to wood and stone", and there was a general obligation to help him and everyone else see the light. When I sang that hymn, I would enjoy the mental images of Greenland's icy mountains and India's coral strand, and I would remember the Chinese idol that sat at that time in my mother's front room, and I would think no more about it.

Let's have a quick look at part of that hymn, and draw out the assumptions which at that time I used to leave unexamined.

> *From Greenland's icy mountains,*
> *From India's coral strand,*
> *Where Afric's sunny fountains*
> *Roll down their golden sand,*
> *From many an ancient river,*
> *From many a palmy plain,*
> *They call us to deliver*
> *Their land from error's chain.*
>
> *Can we, whose souls are lighted*
> *With wisdom from on high,*
> *Can we to men benighted*
> *The lamp of life deny?*
> *Salvation! O salvation!*
> *The joyful sound proclaim,*
> *Till each remotest nation*
> *Has learned Messiah's name.*

And so it goes on. As an anthem for a missionary faith, it is hard to beat. But take a look at the assumptions which lie behind it. We have the truth, everyone else has error. We have the light, everyone else is benighted. In short, we are right, and everyone else is wrong.

It horrifies me now that I accepted that assumption and thought no more about it. Three decades later, I don't accept it any more. This book is partly an attempt to think through the reasons why I don't accept it any more, and partly an attempt to work towards an alternative view that makes sense. It is also an attempt to encourage others to think through the same issues. Not that other people have not been thinking about it, of course. There is a raft of literature on the relationship of Christianity to other faiths, and there are many different ways of thinking about it. But a lot of the argument is conducted between professionals, either in universities and colleges and academic publications, or in dedicated little groups of interfaith enthusiasts. It is conducted by people who already agree that these issues are important, and often it is conducted in specialist language or even in academic jargon, which makes it hard for other people to break into the discussion or get involved. So what I am trying to do is – to borrow an idea from the Heineken advertisements – to reach the parts that other discussions don't reach. If what I write means that these issues are thought about in churches and fellowships and congregations, I'll be happy. If they are discussed in schools, I'll be happy. If they are picked up by study groups and discussion groups, I'll be happy. If they are talked about on the bus and in the bar and spark off letters to the newspaper, I'll be even happier (depending perhaps on the tone of the letters!).

Of course, if there is any reaction, some of it will be from people who very strongly disagree with my conclusions, and I probably won't like it very much. But I hope too that some of it will be from people who are finding that my views help them to form their own, and help them to think carefully through their own position, and I'll be happy with that. That will make it worth while: because I believe myself that this is the most fundamental issue facing not only the Christian churches, not only even the faiths of the world, but the world as a whole. If religions can think through their attitudes to each other, and arrive at some better answers, then the world may even become a better place.

Well, that's enough of the soap-box oratory – for now at least! So let's be clear. This is not an academic book, and it's not founded on three years of uninterrupted study and reading, and it's not going to be full of footnotes and references to learned articles. It's not going to earn me a degree or promotion or letters after my name. It's actually being written in six weeks of study leave from a full-time teaching job, and many aspects of my life have contributed to it. It draws insights from ideas I have encountered reading for degrees in classics and theology, training as a minister and as a teacher of Religious Education, and doing research into a rather obscure aspect of fourth-century Church history. It draws insights from personal experience of thinking, reading, teaching, and above all meeting many different people, especially during the last thirteen years, while I have been in my current job as Head of Religious

Studies and Chaplain in a school which draws its students from many faiths, cultures, and traditions. It is a personal statement of what I have come to see as the way forward, and because it is personal, it will inevitably involve personal anecdotes and stories – as it has already. I am sorry if anyone finds that intrusive or distracting. But it has to be this way, because it is personal experience and personal interaction with others through which we learn. This book is about to become part of your personal experience (unless you are fed up with me already). And whether you agree or disagree, whether you find it helpful or not, this book will help you to form your own views, just as other books have helped me to form mine. Yes, I have read some of the academic books, when I could, and I have talked with many different people about these matters. I have been influenced by many people in many ways, and I cannot always work out how or when; I have absorbed ideas from many books, and I can't always work out which or even necessarily remember reading them (a sign of age, maybe?). So what I have tried to do is give a list of key books at the end which I know have made an impact on me, and that might help those who wish to do so to read further. Most of all, however, I think I have been influenced by the experience over the last ten years of teaching a large number of intelligent and thoughtful young people, of several faiths and of none, about religious studies and the philosophy of religion. The best teaching is not so much a process of imparting knowledge as of working together towards understanding, and in the process the teacher learns too. So to all my students over the last ten years – my thanks! You are partly responsible for who I am!

It is not only classroom encounters with students that have helped me to form my ideas, though. I am not only a teacher of religious studies but also the school Chaplain, with the job of flying the banner of Christian ministry in a school with a large number of students who are committed members of other faiths, in a city whose population is now drawn from a rich variety of cultures, faiths, and backgrounds. In this setting, you cannot avoid the issue of how to relate to those of other faiths; nor can you avoid relating to them in their daily lives, and recognizing the quality of their devotion and the roles that their faith plays in their lives. Once I took this job, there could be neither evasion nor indifference. The issue was going to have to be faced; and over the last twelve years I have been facing it and thinking it through. Let me share with you some of the key elements of the process.

Something that I generally do on entering a new job, or beginning to work with a new group of people, is to work out gradually where my allies are. We all do this, I think, consciously or unconsciously; we look for the people who will be congenial, the people with whom we share ideas and values and enthusiasms, the people with whom we can work and relate easily. On one level it is about the people who share an interest: for instance, who else likes hillwalking (which I do) or football (which I don't)? But on a different level it is a matter of finding out who shares the same vision. Who sees the job the same way I do, and shares the same kind of goals as I do? Who sees the world, the universe, and everything broadly the same way that I do?

Surprising patterns emerged as I gradually worked out who my allies were at the school where I work. Of course there are lots of interlocking patterns, because we humans are complex, and I might see eye to eye with people on some issues and differ extremely on others. But one of the elements in the complex weave of relationships interests me particularly. It became clear to me that the lines were not drawn along lines of religion; the alliances did not emerge in the terms that my great-grandfather might have expected, of Christians over against the rest, or even of one religion over against another. I thought for a while that it was panning out in terms of people of faith over against people of no faith. This is after all a natural alliance; we who are committed to a system of religious belief and practice have something in common which is not shared by those who are not. We tend, at least in the civilized setting of a school, to respect each other's practices and beliefs, and even to make life easy for each other. It has become my responsibility as Chaplain to act as advocate for the Muslim students in negotiations over their prayer room. Similarly, many Muslim parents prefer to send their children to a school with a

Christian ethos, even though it is not their own, than to a secular school with no religious affiliation. I have come across this view many times as an inspector of schools, and this too might lead one to see the natural lines of alliance as those dividing people of faith from people of none. It is similar to the view expressed by Prince Charles when he expressed his views a few years ago on the British royal title "Defender of the Faith", originally granted by the Pope to King Henry the Eighth. The Prince said that he far preferred the general title "Defender of Faith" to the specific "Defender of *the* Faith", and I have a great deal of sympathy with this position.

I did need to modify my views slightly, though, when I got to know my friend Tim, who is head of the Economics department. Tim was brought up a member of the Church of England, and is now a humanist and convinced atheist; and yet our outlooks on life are very similar and in many ways we see eye to eye – so much so that we joke about the teamwork of God and Mammon! Two things play a big part, it seems to me, in my alliance with Tim, apart of course from the fact that he is a nice guy of similar background who, like me, loves his family and enjoys a glass of wine. First, he believes that questions about faith and belief, the ultimate questions about God and the universe, are worth thinking about. Like me, he thinks these are serious matters for thoughtful enquiry, even though we have drawn different conclusions from our thinking. And second, he knows that I am not going to try to browbeat him into thinking what I think. So Tim has taught me that lines of alliance can be drawn up when people respect each other's views and agree on what things are important. I have much more in common with Tim, who would say "I agree with you that this question of God is important, even though I deeply disagree with your views on the question", than I have with the person who says "I think this whole God business is a load of old rubbish and I have no interest in whatever you might think about it". You might have worked out also, by now, that I do not have that much in common with the person who says "I know everything I need to know about God and I know I am right and I know you are wrong".

Among students too, the natural allies were not necessarily only among the Christian students. Within the bounds of those who shared a faith, the alliances tended to be drawn up along the lines of respect towards different views. Again, the Christians who were going all out to convert their friends seemed to have far more in common with the Muslims who were preaching Islam as the final answer to the problems of the Western world, than they did with the Christians who were open to the possibility that God might relate directly even to people of other faiths, or the Muslims who wanted to engage in some serious discussion with their Christian neighbors. It also became apparent to me that the "I'm right, you're wrong" brigade, of whatever faith, were inevitably having a desta-bilizing and disturbing effect on the school community; whereas the "Let's try and understand each other" brigade, of which I was emerging as a figurehead, were having what I think was a stabiliz-ing and community-building effect. So this was a powerful indicator of a good way forward, but I wasn't quite happy with the "Live and let live" approach. Was there a sense in which we were selling out the Christian heritage and ducking out of the obligation to preach the Gospel? These questions have to be faced, and we'll return to them later.

I have been saddened, on both educational and religious grounds, by those students (very few, I am glad to say) who did not wish to learn about beliefs and practices other than their own, and even more so by those parents who wished to deny their children that opportunity. I vividly remember one meeting in which I explained to a parent the educational aims of Religious Studies, drawing on ideas about extending understanding and mutual respect, only to be told that the parent understood what I was saying but did not wish her son to understand or respect beliefs that were wrong! I was saddened that she thought her son had nothing to learn, and by her closed-minded assumption that she had everything sorted out and tied down, and by her judgmental attitude towards oth-ers. Above all it seemed odd to me that a person so confident in the rightness of her own faith and her own beliefs should feel that there was anything to fear from encounter with other views. If you believe that you have the truth, surely you can expect the truth to prevail, or at least to be resistant to challenge? If you are strong in your own faith, surely there can be no threat in learning about other people's?

Alliances and priorities and new understandings were emerging. I was touched, after a few years, to be asked by the father of one of my students to write a foreword to a book he was publishing. Dr Krishan Chopra is a scholar of Sanskrit and had written a book of translation, interpretation, and commentary on the Yajna Mantras, recited during many ceremonies and devotions in Hindu tradition. The book was to be published as part of the centenary celebrations of Gurukul Kangari University at Hardwar in India. Dr Chopra could have asked any number of Indian scholars to write a foreword to his excellent book; and yet he asked me, the Christian chaplain of his son's school. I was delighted to oblige, and I read the work with great interest and learned a lot from it. I wrote in the foreword that Dr Chopra's expositions "touch on many universal themes about the nature of God and of the world, and elucidate complex ideas by means of simple language and easily understood images". And I meant every word of it. I could not regard these scholarly aids to devotion as the product of a faith sunk in ignorance and error. And so yet again I knew that I was going to have to work out a different way of understanding the relationship between my faith and that of other traditions.

One of my Muslim students, at that time quite young and a zealous advocate of Islam, got to hear about this, and came to talk to me about it. He was not entirely happy with the idea that Hindu tradition could have something of value to say about God. He wanted to know whether I thought the same about Islam. Did I believe, he asked, that the words of the Qur'an were the words of God? Here was a dilemma. How was I to respond? I wanted to be true to the beliefs I was developing, that what we call God is far greater than any of our faiths, and is revealed to humans in many ways and through the insights of many traditions. At the same time I did not want to give what would seem to him a flip or glib answer, or to give him something which he could quote out of context and therefore confuse others or misrepresent me. So I said something along the lines that I could not rule out the possibility that God was guiding Muhammad as he has guided others throughout the history of human faith, including Abraham, Moses, and Jesus. Instantly he came back to me: "Then why aren't you a Muslim?" Not a bad question: but the answer came to me just as quickly. Because I do not believe that the Qur'an is the full and final revelation, correct in all things and the final word on the subject of the relationship between God and humanity. I went on to explain my position using my understanding of Islamic belief about the New Testament, so that he would see exactly what I meant. It is mainstream Islamic belief that Jesus was a prophet to whom God revealed truth, and that elements of that truth were recorded by his followers. However his followers also, being human, interpreted their encounter with Jesus in their own terms, and were influenced by their own inherited ideas and assumptions. The result of this was they distorted and corrupted and misunderstood and misinterpreted his teaching, so that in the end the New Testament, according to Islam, contains some material that is trustworthy and much that is not. It contains both truth about God and material that is affected by the culture and assumptions and ideas of the people who put it together. It is not the full and final record of the truth, because it is the product of human efforts to understand and interpret Jesus, and the result of those efforts is inevitably flawed, because humans are not that good at understanding and interpreting God! I was able to tell my pupil that I saw the Qur'an in the same way – as a document which might contain truth about God but also contained material affected by the culture and assumptions and ideas of seventh-century Arabia. It was perhaps valuable data but I did not believe it was the full and final answer, and so I was not a Muslim.

Well, he did not agree, obviously, but he understood what I was driving at, and because he understood it, he respected my position. He was interested, though, to know whether I believed the same about the New Testament: that it was the flawed and culturally conditioned product of human efforts to understand and interpret Jesus. As it happens, I do think that, and told him so. Here I felt

I was on strong ground. My theology degree and my ministerial training had taken me quite some distance from the Bible class days when "because the Bible says so" was a knock-down answer. I had learned to ask in what context, and for what reason, the Bible says so. I had learned to try to understand the culture and assumptions of the writers of the different scriptural books, and to try to draw out their original intention and meaning – scholars call this exegesis. I had learned to try to work out how these insights could be applied to our vastly different situation as twenty-first century believers – this one is hermeneutics. And I had learned that these are complex and subtle skills, and that the glib production of a one-line quotation – a "proof-text" – without attention to context or intention was not an appropriate way of using the wisdom of the scriptural writers. So I was happy for the moment with the position established. It does of course flag up the vital importance of working out one's attitude to Scripture before one tackles these questions of different faiths, and we shall return to this question in greater detail in chapter seven. For now, let's just note that before you use Scripture as an authority or as the basis for an argument, you have to work out your attitude to it. Fortunately, in studying theology and in training for the ministry, I had already developed my approach to Scripture before ever considering the matter of other faiths.

Mind you, later on, when my young Muslim student had grown up a bit, and was studying for his A levels, and had gained a bit of expertise in the philosophy of religion, he spotted one of the difficulties in the position I was tentatively developing, and which I had tried to explain to him. He agreed that the New Testament was a mixture of different kinds of material. He agreed that it contained some material which was true and relevant for all time, and some material which was culturally conditioned, founded on false or outdated assumptions, or just plain wrong. He liked to challenge me with the question of how I could decide which was which. Into which category did any given bit of New Testament teaching fall? It is easy of course for a Muslim to answer that question about the Christian Scriptures. If Biblical teaching agrees with the teaching of the Qur'an, which fortunately is much more unitary than the Bible, then it is true; if it does not, then it is false. The Muslim can use the Qur'an as a yardstick to judge Christian teaching, and believes it to be an infallible tool. But how could I judge, he asked. I had no infallible yardstick. I had only reason and tradition and scholarship; and I had already agreed that all these were likely to produce flawed results. My understanding could be no more than provisional.

He was right, of course. And he always used to be a little taken aback when I seemed to have no problem with that. He did not like the idea of a provisional understanding. And yet I do believe that is what we have. Further, I believe that the sooner we admit that all our religious understandings are provisional, that we do not have the full and final answers, the better ground we shall have for moving forward in a positive relationship, and learning from each other. We shall also of course have removed any grounds that any of us might have had for imposing our understanding on others, or insisting that they must conform to our way of seeing things. We shall have removed completely from play the way my great-grand-father thought, for we shall be forced to abandon or at the very least radically redefine the missionary task. We shall also have revised yet again the symbolism attached to my Chinese ancestor figure. He began in a family shrine as a symbol of veneration for the ancestors and of family piety. He became a symbol of conversion when he was handed over, and he became a symbol of a missionary job well done for my own forebears. Now he has become for me a symbol of all the questions that need asking before we try to impose our will and our understanding on people born and brought up with wholly different beliefs. He sits there, mutely questioning the assumption that one faith has the right to do that to another. He stimulates the conscience and the intellect to come up with a clear understanding of how faiths relate to each other.

He stands as a symbol of all the influences and experiences which have left me believing that we need to shift, in effect, from a situation in which all of us see our own faith as superior to others, to one in which we treat each other as equals. Not equally right nec-essarily – we'll come back to this too – but equal in admitting that though we may have got a lot of things right, we may equally have got some things wrong. Equal in admitting that our best efforts to explain and clarify and state our beliefs and understandings are only provisional. Equal in admitting that each of us has only reached a limited and provisional stage in unraveling an understanding of the great mystery that is God, or Reality, or Transcendence, or whatever other provisional label we come up with.

There are huge implications to all this, of course, and you are probably jumping up and down with frustration at all the questions that arise. But I hope that has made you want to read further; because the rest of this book will be trying to back up the assertions made here, and to go into some of the implications in greater depth. It will start by examining some of the different possible ways of understanding relationships between faiths, and drawing out what is attractive and what is less so about each of them. That will explain in a more systematic way how I have ended up at the position for which I am arguing here, and give you a chance to think it through for yourself too.

2

We are right,
you are wrong

This is the traditional view which we have already met in the missionary world of my great-grandfather, and which has been a dominant view through much of the history of Christianity. It is the view which teaches that only Christianity has the truth about God. Only through a relationship with Jesus Christ can a human being be in a right relationship with God, and so obtain personal fulfillment and salvation. This is the position which has become known over the last twenty years in academic circles as *exclusivism*, because it believes that the Christian faith is the exclusive road, the one and only road, to understanding of God and to a fulfilled life. The message about other faiths here is clear. They do not do the business. Their claims are false, their teachings are misleading, the efforts of their followers are futile and doomed to failure. The followers of other faiths are not serving God in any positive sense. They are either following and praying to an imaginary being who does not exist – to a non-God; or they are trying to follow God in so mistaken and perverse a fashion that there is no value in what they do. They are *excluded* from salvation or from understanding of the truth.

Exclusivist understandings of course vary. Protestants have tended to lay stress on acknowledging Jesus Christ as Lord and Savior, whereas the Catholic tradition has tended to emphasize baptism and membership of the visible Church. Either way the message is the same: outside Christianity, the ultimate outlook is bleak. As the Roman Catholics used to put it, "Extra Ecclesiam Nulla Salus" – "Outside the Church there is no salvation" – which at its mediaeval strongest was applied to mean that outside the Roman Catholic Church there was no salvation, and was even used to exclude the members of other churches! Roman Catholics no longer take such a dim view of other Christians, and more recently the Roman Catholic Church has officially moved away from a rigidly exclusivist view of other faiths. However this view is still extremely well represented in modern Christianity. Outsiders are seen as being in error, living by false teachings as opposed to true, stumbling in darkness as opposed to walking in the light of Christ.

How is it justified? Usually it is by reference to Scripture. In the New Testament there are many texts which can be taken at face value to show that there is no way to a proper relationship with God except through the faith of the followers of Jesus. Examples are easily found:

> "I am the way, the truth, and the life: no one comes to the
> Father except by me."   John 14.6

> "There is salvation in no one else, for there is no other
> name under heaven given among men by which we must
> be saved."   Acts 4.12

If it is a knock-down argument to say "The Bible Says" and then produce a text like this, then the grounds for exclusivism are pretty solid. And if this is not enough, then the Bible has some pretty tough things to say about those who follow other faiths:

> "Do not try to work together as equals with unbelievers,
> for it cannot be done. How can right and wrong be
> partners? How can light and darkness live together? How
> can Christ and the Devil agree? What does a believer have
> in common with an unbeliever? How can God's temple
> come to terms with pagan idols?"   2 Corinthians 6.14–16

Again, if we are playing proof-texts, here is a knock-down argument for regarding all non-Christians as unbelievers who live in darkness, who are led astray by the devil, who are – in short – wrong. It is interesting, though, that it is possible to quote proof-texts that seem to point the other way too. Try Peter in Caesarea, as he learns not to make distinctions between Jews and Gentiles, or to think that any person is ritually unclean or defiled:

> "I now realize that it is true that God treats everyone on the same basis. Whoever worships him and does what is right is acceptable to him, no matter what race he belongs to."   Acts 10.34

or this, with its emphasis on what is *done*:

> "Not every one that calls to me 'Lord, Lord' shall enter the kingdom of heaven, but those who do the will of my father who is in heaven."   Matthew 7.21

And I have always rather liked this one, which is Jesus' response to his disciples trying to stop someone casting out demons, because he was not one of their group:

> "Do not stop him: for whoever is not against you is for you."   Luke 9.50

The only trouble with this is that if you go onwards a few chapters, you find the opposite sentiment expressed by Jesus:

> "He who is not with me is against me."   Luke 11.23

The upshot of all this, of course, is to expose the futility and even the foolishness of arguing by the proof-text. We need to ask, in the case of the last two, exactly what it meant in each case to be against Jesus or for Jesus. We need to try to understand the text by looking at the context and the intention of the writer and the teaching point that is being made. And of course we need to do exactly the same with the texts that seem to back up the exclusivist position, and we shall do in due course.

For the moment however it is enough to note the kind of Scriptural text which is used to back up the exclusivist position. Clearly Christians who take this view will be very keen to evangelize, to preach the good news and to attempt to convert people to the true faith. The only decent thing you can do if you have the truth is to commend it to others. The logic of this cannot be faulted, and the motivation for missionary work can be both understood and applauded.

So what's the problem? Why is it that many Christians do not feel any more that this is the right way to see the relationship between Christianity and other faiths?

The first thing to note is that for many of us, once we have begun to live and work among people who belong to other faiths, and once we have begun to learn something about them, this view simply does not fit with our experience. Many of those whom we meet seem to be very like ourselves in their loyalty and devotion to their faith, in the honor they give to its requirements, and in their efforts to live in this complex world in a way that is faithful to their tradition. Many indeed put us to shame by their reverence and prayerfulness. It is very hard to see such people as benighted heathen, doomed to hellfire, when one can see in them so many admirable and enviable qualities.

It is not just the quality of their devotion or their loyalty, though. When Matthew records Jesus warning his followers against false prophets, he records the guidance Jesus gives, to help them distinguish the false from the true: "by their fruits you shall know them" (Matthew 7.16). The teaching goes on with the kind of simple image which is often found in the Gospels: a good tree cannot bear evil fruit, and an evil tree cannot bear good fruit. It is a simple and easy test: and it is a test which many non-Christians pass. It is not hard to think of members of other faiths who stand as shining examples for the good effects of their lives on those around them, whether on the world stage like Mahatma Gandhi, or on the local stage like the devout Hindu or Muslim or Jewish neighbors who live alongside many of us.

This is not to claim of course that all Hindus or Muslims or Jews are shining examples – but then not all Christians are either. Most of us are doing our best, but falling far short of the standards to which we aspire. Most of us bear something of a mixture of good and rotten fruit. Many of us can be spectacularly fine ambassadors for our faith in some contexts, and spectacularly poor ones in others. It may depend upon mood, or on what else is going on in our lives at the time. Most of us can be good Samaritans now and again, but all too often be like the people who passed by on the other side. In this respect we are all pretty much alike, whether we are Christian or not. And yet if the exclusivist position were right, there ought to be something outstanding about Christians. It ought to be possible to tell Christians apart by the quality of their lives, by the fruits of their faith. Can we honestly claim that that is the case?

If we look at the guidance given in the letter to the Galatians about the fruits of the Spirit, things do not get any easier. According to this well-known list, the fruits of the Spirit are "love, joy, peace, longsuffering, gentleness, goodness, faith, meekness, temperance". (Galatians 5.22–23). Certainly there are Christians who are fine examples of a life marked by these characteristics. But equally there are many who struggle with them, just as the people of the Galatian church themselves did, for the letter implies that many of them were exhibiting quite different kinds of behavior! Equally there are many members of other faiths who put the faltering efforts of many Christians to shame, and exhibit exactly these qualities, and have respect for them from within and beyond their faith community. In all religious groups, it is a pretty mixed picture. One is left with the feeling that whatever good qualities may be seen in Christians, they are equally to be seen in followers of other faiths; and whatever bad qualities may be seen in some followers of other faiths, they are pretty well represented among Christians too. So in terms of the fruits we bear, of lifestyle and devotion and reverence, it is very hard for any faith to claim the moral high ground over against any other.

This feeling is backed up by the simple reflection that for most of us, the faith to which we owe allegiance is the result of a particular accident of birth and upbringing. It used to be possible to say that those who were born in a particular place would have a particular set of beliefs; but this does not work any more. Family and community still play a huge part; so it can easily happen that of three children born in the same city hospital and brought up in the same city area, one will be Christian, one Muslim, one Sikh, because that is the faith and the cultural heritage of the family into which they were born. Is it really so straightforward to claim that out of those three children, one is fortunate enough to be heading for salvation, thanks to the lucky circumstances of birth, whereas the others are headed for damnation unless they have the good fortune to be converted from the faith of their family? In one case, if we think like this, loyalty is rewarded; in the others, loyalty is punished. In one case, devotion to the faith of the family is to be encouraged; in the others it is to be condemned, overturned, uprooted.

At the very least these considerations raise serious questions about the "We are right, you are wrong" approach, and should lead us to wonder whether there are other approaches which might be preferable. Other important questions which are often raised when this approach is discussed concern the fate of various defined groups of people. What about those who lived before the coming of Jesus? In particular what about the Jewish people, who have the special status in their own tradition, recognized in Christian scripture and tradition too, as God's chosen, covenant people? What about the great philosophers of ancient Greece, on whose teaching so much developed Christian theology depends? What about those who have never heard the Gospel? What about those who cannot understand enough about it to respond to it? What about the sincere and honest unbeliever? The exclusivist approach of course has developed various ways of dealing with these questions; but they keep on being asked. Can we really believe that the God to whom the life and death of Jesus bear witness is the kind of God who will condemn a large part of his creation just for being unlucky enough to be born at the wrong time, or in the wrong place, or with the virtue of loyalty and devotion that happens to be misplaced? What are the underlying beliefs about God which go along with the "We are right, you are wrong" approach? And are we prepared to accept them?

These are serious questions. Yet for me there is an even more important line of questioning: and that concerns the attitudes and actions which can only too easily arise from this approach. In any other area of life, the exclusivist attitude would be called judgmental and condemnatory; and it is sad but true that an attitude of judgment can too easily go alongside exclusivism. We have seen how the exclusivist approach is a powerful motivator for mission; and you cannot get away from the fact that the missionary approach passes judgment on the beliefs, traditions, and loyalties of those whom it sets out to convert. The missionary hymns in my grandfather's "Methodist Tune Book" are revealing: glorious and stirring to sing, no doubt, and certainly forthright in their approach to the beliefs of others. In the "Missions at Home and Abroad" section, no. 809, "Let the song go round the earth" includes the verse:

> *Let the song go round the earth,*
> *Lands where Islam's sway*
> *Darkly broods o'er home and hearth*
> *Cast their bonds away;*
> *Let His praise from Afric's shore*
> *Rise and swell her wide lands o'er.*

No messing about there. It is no surprise that the next section is "The Church Militant and Triumphant". It is still in the Mission section that we find "March we forth in the strength of God, with the banner of Christ unfurled"; but by the time we get to "The Son of God goes forth to War" or Baring Gould's glorious "Onward! Christian Soldiers, Marching as to War", we are definitely in the militant and triumphant section. And yet the Church has somehow never been at her most attractive or most like Jesus when at her most militant and triumphant. The military metaphor is not without its value of course; there is a lot of good imagery in the "battle" between good and evil, light and darkness, justice against injustice, and the military metaphor leads to the natural question "Which side are we on?" Yet it also tends to lead to militaristic thinking, and a militant approach to others, and to religious conflict.

Are we really in the business of encouraging conflict? I would argue strongly that in the interests of community, nation, and world, we ought to be resolving conflict where possible, arguing for peace, and working for respect and understanding between nations and ethnic groups – and, yes, between religious groups too. Yet all too often where the attitude is "We are right, you are wrong", there is anything but peace. All too often, the next step after "You are wrong" is "and we have the right to impose our beliefs on you and to discourage your beliefs". And from that step come tragic consequences. It is not hard to think of atrocities committed by one religious group against another, or against a world dominated by other values, either in our own century or in past ones. There are few faiths without guilty episodes, and they always spring from "We are right, you are wrong", with the extension – "and because of this, we have the right to impose our rightness on you by force, or make you aware of it by terror".

You will often hear people who have rejected religious belief talk about the evils which have been done in the name of religion, and the wars and atrocities which have been caused at least in large part by religion. They will talk about the Spanish Inquisition, and they will talk about the Crusades, and they will talk about the partition of India, and they will talk about 9/11. They have no shortage of examples, and even if there are often more complex causes at work than they admit, the root cause is usually the kind of religion that says "We are right, you are wrong", and then adopts a militant attitude towards those who are wrong.

Of course I am not saying that every exclusivist is a militant: but it is at least an occupational hazard of this kind of attitude towards the beliefs of others. It is an attitude that is cast into question by such elements of Gospel tradition as "Blessed are the peacemakers" and the rest of the Beatitudes (Matthew 5.3–11), which say nothing about being right and quite a lot about humility and the desire for righteousness, and even more perhaps by the punchy warning of Matthew 7.1: "Judge not, that you be not judged". Are we so sure that we have everything right, in our particular tradition, with our particular understanding, in our particular time and place, that we can afford to sit in judgment on others?

If the answer to that question is "maybe not", then we need to look further, and see if we can find an approach that is more generous, more positive, and more likely to give us a good reason to work positively, peacefully, and respectfully with those of other faiths, without betraying our own. That way we may be able to find a rationale for working together for the good of all of us.

3

We are right, you have made a good start

When you first look at it, this view has a much more friendly flavor about it. From my point of view as a teacher, it reminds me of the kind of thing I tend to say to a student who has not entirely got the drift of what is going on, but whose answer gives some glimmer of hope that he may be latching on to something useful. I don't want to discourage him by telling him he is wrong, but equally I can't tell him he is right when he isn't! So I try to use some kind of friendly and encouraging phrase like "you've made a good start on thinking about that", "you're getting there" or "you're going in the right direction". I used to say "you're working towards a good answer there" – but that one has been slightly discredited by the educational habit of using "working towards" to mean "has not yet achieved". In a report, to say "Johnny is working towards level one" really means "Johnny has not even achieved level one yet"! But I digress, and I am sure you get the point. This attitude has a much more encouraging flavor at first sight.

This way of thinking is a response in part to some of those nasty questions we raised about the "we're right, you're wrong" approach. We noted that it is very hard to say baldly to the Jews "You are wrong", when so much Christian teaching and understanding springs directly out of Judaism, and Christianity acknowledges the special covenant relationship which was and is at the heart of the Jewish sense of identity. We noted too that it was hard to say that followers of pre-Christian faiths were plain wrong, when – to be blunt – those faiths were all that was around at the time.

This approach takes these questions seriously, and indeed takes its foundation from the attitude of the early Church to Judaism. Christianity sprang out of Judaism, and had its original nucleus in the Jewish following of a wandering Jewish teacher. As it began to develop a separate identity and moved out into the Gentile world as well, the new movement had to define its relationship with Judaism quickly. As the book of Acts shows, some of the apostles, like Peter, retained a strong sense of their own Jewish roots and loyalties, and continued worshipping in the synagogues as long as it was practical for them to do so. Even Paul, who was a key figure in the Gentile mission and in the expansion of the new faith through the Eastern Mediterranean, clearly retained his pride in his Jewish upbringing and scholarly training, as we can see from his references to them in Philippians chapter three. He and his companions must have given much thought to the relationship of the new movement to the Jewish faith; and their conclusions are pretty clear in various places in the New Testament. Matthew, who has a special interest in Jewish matters, has Jesus explaining where he stands in relation to the Law of Moses, which he seems at times to be challenging or re-defining:

> "Do not think I am come to destroy the law or the prophets: I am come not to destroy but to fulfill."
>
> **Matthew 5.17**

And fulfillment, in this sense, is a constant theme of the evangelists and the other New Testament writers. From his birth as a descendant of David to his announcement by John the Baptist, from his miracles and mighty works to his suffering and humiliation, from his entry into Jerusalem on a donkey to his execution outside the city on a cross, Jesus is presented as fulfilling the prophecies of the prophets of Israel. Moses and Elijah are recorded as appearing beside him at the Transfiguration, to show that both the Law and the

Prophets – that is, the entire religion of the people of Israel – are brought to fulfillment in Jesus. Judaism was not wrong; it was a good start, a preparation for its fulfillment in Jesus. It was partial understanding and partial insight; in Christ, understanding and insight were made complete.

So God had indeed been dealing with the Jewish people over the long period of their history, from Abraham and Isaac and Jacob, through Moses and the Exodus, and through the Prophets who called the people to be faithful; but all of this had been leading up to the coming of Jesus and the fulfillment of God's purpose. The relationship is made explicit in the beginning of the letter to the Hebrews:

> "In the past, God spoke to our ancestors many times and
> in many ways through the prophets, but in these last
> days he has spoken to us through his Son... He (the Son)
> reflects the brightness of God's glory and is the exact
> likeness of God's own being, sustaining the universe with
> his powerful word..."   **Hebrews I.I–3**

The message is clear: you had the start, we have the finish. You were working towards, we have achieved. Your faith has a great deal of value: but it has this value precisely because it is leading to ours. You are the preparation, we are the fulfillment. It is a positive and indeed a necessary role for Judaism: but the differential is preserved in favor of Christianity.

The book of Acts tells of St Paul adopting a similar view of some elements of Greek religion in his missionary work in Athens, when he speaks to the ancient council of the Areopagus, where he has been summoned to explain his activities. He does not begin by telling the Athenians that they are wrong, or that they are sunk in pagan superstition and the darkness of idol-worship. Instead he finds something to build on – a connection with something in their own experience that might help them make sense of what he is saying. He even commends them for their interest in religious matters. And he finds the link with what he wants to say in the altar he has found in the city inscribed "To an Unknown God".

Now he could have had a really good go at them over this. For it is likely that this altar was set up as part of the popular habit of keeping on the right side of as many gods as possible. Many people in the cities of the Eastern Roman Empire at this time tended to collect membership of cults in much the same way as some people today sign up to lots of insurance policies – the more you have, the better your chances of being covered against disaster. In Athens, or Alexandria, or Ephesus, some people felt that the more gods you kept on the right side of, the better your chances were of attaining whatever you were looking for in this life or the next. And it would seem that one group had hedged its bets even more. They had decided to set up an altar to an unknown god, just in case they had missed out some god of whom they had not heard, and therefore upset that god.

Paul could have said plenty about this. He could have told them that you can't "pick-and-mix" your religion. He could have told them this was nothing but superstition, or that you couldn't buy your way to salvation by staying on the right side of the gods. As a Jew and a follower of the Christ, he would have been horrified by the use of multiple idols in worship – as indeed Acts 17.16 says he was. But he did not choose to go down this road. Instead, as we have seen, he praised them for their interest in religion, and for worshipping an unknown God: and then he told them all about the unknown God. "That which you worship, then, even though you do not know it, is what I now proclaim to you." (Acts 17.24) He has found something in this rather unpromising Greek superstition, which seems to have prepared the people to hear the word of the Gospel. There is something which he can regard as preparing the ground for preaching the full message of Jesus Christ. Even in Greek superstition there is preparation for the Gospel. We are right, but they have made a good start.

Others in the early Church found more ground for regarding Greek philosophy, rather than Greek religion, as preparation for the Gospel. As Christianity spread beyond the Jewish communities, educated in the Law and the Prophets, to cultured Gentiles educated in the literature and philosophy of the Greeks, these educated folk found that Christian teaching fitted in very well with much that they had learned from their philosophical reading. Socrates had challenged the superstition of popular Greek religion, and focused his mind on enquiring after what might make a man virtuous. His disciple Plato had developed ideas about the eternal, unchanging nature of Ideals like Truth, Justice, Beauty, and above all Goodness, and had taught at times about a creator God. Some of Plato's followers by the first century had already linked the Ideals with the figure of God to come up with the idea of one divine figure who summed up all the eternal virtues in himself. With ideas of this kind circulating in the intellectual world of the Greeks, it is easy to see how educated converts came to believe that their philosophy had been a preparation for receiving the Gospel, and it was only a short step from that to the belief that God had inspired the philosophers of Greece, like the prophets of Israel, to lay a foundation for the coming of Christ. It was now possible to say not only to the Jewish faith but to the philosophical tradition of the Greeks, "We are right, but you're getting there; you've made a good start; you're working towards the truth quite nicely".

This gives an attractive option to many Christians who are put off by the negativity of the "you're wrong" approach. Just as I do not want to respond negatively to the efforts of a student to come up with a good answer, even if he hasn't quite managed to do so, many Christians do not want to respond negatively to the sincerely held beliefs of people of other faiths. But of course they still want to preserve the differential for Christianity. So to view other faiths positively as helping prepare the ground for Christianity is quite an attractive option. They can be regarded as asking the right questions, or raising awareness of the right issues, or encouraging the right attitudes. Other faiths can now be regarded as moving in the right kind of direction, even if they don't get as far. They are fellow-travelers, even if their map is rather inferior and we feel they would do better if they moved on to work from ours instead.

A huge virtue of this approach for many Christians is that it is built on an attitude which is found, as we have seen, in Scripture (though I have heard a hard-line exclusivist maintain that Paul's

Areopagus speech was his least successful bit of missionary work in Acts, and that the fact he made so few converts shows us that this is a bad attitude to take!). It is commendable in its positive view that other faiths have at least some value. It gives a better flavor to missionary work, which can now be seen not so much as an instruction to abandon the old and replace it with the new, but as an invitation to build upon the old and move forward to fuller understanding.

Nevertheless, some problems remain. It is not as easy as it seems to build a general approach to other faiths on the basis of this attitude. It certainly worked quite well for Christians looking at the Jewish faith in the first century, and one can see quite well the argument for treating the work of the philosophers as preparation for the Gospel. One can see too the attraction of the Areopagus-style approach to missionary preaching. And in modern times it works quite well in hindsight. Converts can look back at their previous faith, and from the perspective of Christianity they can say that their previous faith was a preparation. It was a positive influence in their lives, it helped to form them and sensitize them to spiritual matters, until in the end they became aware that they needed to move on to Christianity. I remember a convert from the Sikh faith coming in to speak at my theological college and talking in very much this way, and it was a moving and positive account of a natural progression.

However, these approaches all have one thing in common: that they are seeing the 'other' faith from the viewpoint of Christianity. It is still a case of Christians pronouncing judgment on others, from the Christian point of view. There are two problems with this. One is the obvious problem that once again there is the danger of smugness or arrogance – that is a common problem with all the approaches that begin with "We are right". But if we are aware of the danger, and we are people of goodwill, we can at least try to resist any tendency to come across in this way. More serious is the problem that to regard other faiths as no more than a preparation for Christianity is to ride roughshod over their own ways of understanding themselves. It is an easy judgment to make on a faith from outside it. Even a convert from a faith, who still feels pride and loyalty and affection towards the faith of his upbringing, has become an outsider. From inside, things look different. From inside, a faith will not feel like a preparation for something else, but like an authentic way of life and system of belief in its own right.

It is hard to maintain this viewpoint in the face of the devotion and dedication of many ordinary followers of Judaism today, who have a full and satisfying and authentic life within their ancient and complex tradition. It does not feel to them like a preparation for something else; and if Christians are to make a judgment about a faith which is quite alien to the followers of that faith, then they need to be careful.

And what of the faiths which come later in the history of religion? If it is hard to maintain that Judaism *today* still has its preparatory character, it is even harder to maintain this of the faiths whose origin is more recent. What of Islam, which treats Christianity as a misunderstanding of the teaching of the prophet Jesus, whom Muslims believe preached (among other things) about the coming of the Prophet Muhammad? What of the Sikh faith, founded by Guru Nanak as a means of reconciling the traditions of Islam and Indian spirituality? It would be far easier to say that Hindu and Islamic traditions were preparations for their fulfillment in the Sikh faith, than to say that all of them are preparations awaiting their fulfillment in Christianity; and yet that too would be a distortion of Islamic or Hindu self-understanding. That too would be to make a judgment from a different perspective and impose it from outside.

So we seem to have an attractive approach to other faiths, which worked particularly well in some first-century contexts, and works quite well as an account of the journey of believing in the lives of some individuals, but does not adapt very well into a general attitude to help Christians approach other faiths now. It also does not appear to be very helpful in giving the members of different faiths a common ground for working together, because there is still very little shared ground. Christians may see believers in other faiths as seeking in the right kind of direction, or asking the right questions, but they will see the direction as ultimately defined by Christianity, and the answers to the questions as being ultimately the Christian ones. The believers themselves, on the other hand, will see their own faiths as not only asking questions but also giving answers. They will not see them as preparation for something else but as authentic and complete in their own right. While there is such a difference of viewpoint, it is hard to see how there is shared ground on which to stand.

We have, then, two major problems in using this viewpoint as a way of defining the relationship between Christianity and other faiths. Both arise from the fact that Christianity is seen as functioning on a superior level to all the others. Everything else is preparation; Christianity is fulfillment. Everything else may be judged from the Christian perspective, and is inevitably found to be lacking. This is not really a very good basis for a partnership or collaboration; and yet as we have noted, the faiths have to collaborate and work together if conflict and mutual hostility, with all their dire consequences, are to be avoided. So once again we need to look further. It is beginning to look as though we may need to find some way of avoiding Christians sitting in judgment on other faiths. Both the main problems we have identified could be avoided by seeing Christianity as somehow on the same level as the other faiths, rather than adopting a smug and superior viewpoint. We'll have to come back to this idea; but before then, let's consider one more very attractive and popular way of seeing the value and the goodness in other faiths.

4

We are right, you are partly right (even if you don't know it)

Yes, it's a long chapter title this time; but then it's quite a hard idea to distil into a single phrase. Let's start examining it by having a look at one of C S Lewis' excellent "Narnia" books. I hope you are familiar with these, and not just from the film and TV versions. They are fine stories in their own right, and thought-provoking allegories of Christian teaching as well.

Lewis tackles the issue of other faiths in the seventh and last book of the series, "The Last Battle", which also offers views on the questions of death, judgment, afterlife, and the destiny of the world – as well as wrapping up the stories of all the characters in all the preceding six books! The part that concerns us falls quite near the end of the book, in the chapter entitled "Farther Up and Farther In". There have been two main groups of believers in the book: the people of Narnia, who follow the divine Lion Aslan (Aslan is the figure representing Jesus in Lewis' allegorical version of Christianity), and the people of Calormen, who worship the demonic figure Tash. One of the Calormenes, Emeth, is a rather sympathetic figure: a good, kindly figure with high ethical standards and a burning devotion to Tash, in whose service he has done much good. In this extract he tells the story – in the rather archaic language which Lewis uses to represent Calormene speech – of his encounter at judgment with Aslan:

> "Then I fell at his feet and thought, Surely this is the hour
> of death, for the Lion (who is worthy of all honor) will
> know that I have served Tash all my days and not him.
> ... But the Glorious One bent down his golden head and
> touched my forehead and said, Son, thou art welcome.
> But I said, Alas, Lord, I am no son of thine but the servant
> of Tash. He answered, Child, all the service thou hast
> done to Tash, I account as service done to me."

Emeth inquires further, and is told that all true and good service is
in fact service done to Aslan:

> "If any man swear by Tash and keep his oath for the oath's
> sake, it is by me that he has truly sworn, though he know
> it not, and it is I who reward him."

But Emeth feels still constrained to be honest and upfront about his
service to Tash:

> "But I said also (for the truth constrained me), yet I have
> been seeking Tash all my days. Beloved, said the Glorious
> One, unless thy desire had been for me thou wouldst not
> have sought so long and so truly. For all find what they
> truly seek."

The key phrase here is "though he know it not". Emeth thought he
was serving Tash and seeking to learn more of Tash; but in fact,
without knowing it, he was serving Aslan. Here Lewis has planted
in the minds of many readers both a positive approach to all that
is good and honest and worthy in the followers of other faiths,
and a warning to Christians who are tempted to do what is cruel
or unworthy in the name of Christ. He has given readers grounds
to think that followers of other faiths who are truly and sincerely
seeking after their understanding of God are in fact seeking after
Christ without knowing it. They are Christian without being aware
of it. In a phrase to which we shall return shortly, they are "anonymous" Christians. At the same time, he has opened up the opposite

possibility: that people who believe themselves to be Christian may in fact be serving other ideals altogether:

> "And if any man do a cruelty in my name, then, though he says the name Aslan, it is Tash whom he serves and by Tash his deed is accepted."

This is a strong statement of the "By their fruits you shall know them" principle, and it is well worth taking seriously. It has good New Testament backing: for instance, consider the parable of the Sheep and the Goats, which is to be found in Matthew chapter twenty-five and which clearly influenced much of Lewis' portrayal of the Judgment. In this parable there are surprises both for those who believe themselves to be on the right side, and those who do not. When the selection is made and the righteous are divided from the unrighteous, the righteous are surprised to be there because they did not realize they had been serving Jesus. At the same time, the unrighteous are equally surprised, because they do not realize that they have been failing. This is a clear warning that what we believe may not in fact be the case. We may have got things wrong without knowing it. But equally, there may be people who have got things right without knowing it. If this approach is right, then it may be true, as Jesus warns in Matthew 7.21, that "not everyone who calls to me 'Lord, Lord' will enter the Kingdom of Heaven"; but conversely it may also be that some who have never called Jesus 'Lord' may still enter, if they have been following him without knowing it.

There have always been Christians who have found this kind of view attractive, and right from the earliest days they have asked how a person can be a follower of Jesus without knowing it. How does this work? The clue for many lies in the insight that the divine Christ-figure of developed Christian theology, the glorious Son of God, is considerably greater and more complex than the human Jesus. This is the kind of idea that the gospel-writer John was hinting at in the first section of his Gospel. John seems to have come from a different background from Matthew, Mark, and Luke, and to be writing for a readership which was familiar with some of the ideas of Greek philosophy. In his prologue he draws both on Greek ideas and on Jewish tradition:

> "In the beginning was the Logos, and the Logos was
> with God, and the Logos was God. This Logos was in the
> beginning with God. All things were made through him,
> and without him was not anything made that was made.
> In him was life, and the life was the light of men. And
> the light shines in the darkness, and the darkness has not
> overcome it...This was the true light, that enlightens every
> man, coming into the world."   John 1.1–5, 9

This passage is so packed with ideas that scholars can write books just on these few verses. But let's have a go at unpacking the bits that matter to us. First of all, the word Logos is a Greek word which means both "Word" and "Reason", and this will become important. It is usually translated "Word" in English versions of the Gospel, because John begins, quoting the first words of the book of Genesis, by linking his Logos with the creative Word of God by which Genesis chapter one says everything was created: "And God *said*, Let there be light." He goes on of course to identify Jesus as the incarnation of the Logos: "And the Logos became flesh and dwelt among us, and we beheld his glory, glory as of the only-begotten of the Father, full of grace and truth." (John 1.14) So already for John's readers, Jesus is not just the wandering preacher of the Judaean highways and byways, or even the chosen Messiah of the House of David, but the incarnation of the Logos who has been with God from the beginning of time, and was instrumental in creating the heavens and the earth. The Logos is greater than the human Jesus.

And the Logos also has the function of enlightening every human being in the world, in all times and in all places. Whatever is true, whatever is of God, in whatever time, comes to humans by the power of the Logos. Those early Christians who were well tutored in Greek scholarship could easily make a further step, suggested by the double meaning of the word "Logos", and suggest that there was a link between the Logos of God and the faculty of reason which had been given to humans as a gift of God in creation. A second-century scholar, Justin the Martyr, developed this idea fully as he sought to account for the excellent preparation for Christianity given by Socrates, Plato, and their successors. He suggested that it was by the use of their own reason (logos with a small L) that they had been able to gain insight into the Logos (Logos with a capital L) and therefore give others some clues to the truth.

This is a very attractive idea. No longer does it matter that some people were born before the ministry of Jesus, or have never heard the Good News. No longer do the good and sincere and devoted followers of other faiths have to be excluded from the possibility of salvation because they have not known Jesus. The possibility is raised that they have known Jesus, without being aware of it, because they have been inspired by the Logos. They have sought after truth, and such truth as they have found is the truth given by the Logos, that enlightens every true seeker after truth, wherever and whenever they may be. All the attractive features of the belief and practice and devotion of Jew, Muslim, Hindu, Sikh, or whomever else, can be attributed to their being brought into the truth, at least partly, by the power of the Logos. In so far as they have been brought into the truth, then they are followers of the Logos; which means that they are Christians, even though they do not know it.

This is a view that worked well in the multi-faith society of the first and second centuries in the Eastern Roman Empire, and it has not been forgotten. It was adapted by scholars in the twentieth century to meet the challenges of an increasingly multi-faith society in Western Europe, and is now known in the trade by the name of "inclusivism" – an obvious contrast to the "exclusivism" which we have already examined. Inclusivist theology agrees with the exclusivist claim that all salvation is through Jesus Christ; but like the Logos theology, inclusivist theology believes that Christ is not limited by the boundaries of the Christian church. Inclusivists are happy to recognize that God is at work, and the Spirit is active, within the lives of those who follow other religious traditions. Muslims or Jews, Hindus or Sikhs, may be among the followers of the truth that is Jesus Christ, even thought they do not realize it and certainly would not agree to describe it in those terms.

This is the position which is taken up in the central document on this issue produced in 1965 by the Second Vatican Council of the Roman Catholic Church. At this time the Church was seeing the need to adopt a more positive and conciliatory view towards other faiths, and with Vatican Two it made the official move towards inclusivism from its traditional exclusivist position. The document is usually known, according to Roman Catholic custom, by the first two words of its official Latin version: "Nostra Aetate" (In Our Age) – though its full title is "The Declaration on the Relation of the Church to Non-Christian Religions". (We'll stick with "Nostra Aetate"!) The document adopts a respectful tone towards other world faiths, praising the key players for their spiritual achievements and recognizing them as responses to the "profound mysteries of the human condition". It picks up the idea of the Gospel of John and of the Logos theology, acknowledging that the mainstream faiths contain elements of "the truth that enlightens every human being". And in a passage which is often quoted, and with good reason, Nostra Aetate affirms:

> "The Catholic Church rejects nothing which is true and holy in these religions. She looks with sincere respect upon those ways of conduct and of life, those rules and teachings which, though differing in many particulars from what she holds and sets forth, nevertheless often reflect a ray of that Truth which enlightens all men."

This is a huge change from the old exclusivist position, and is largely dependent on the crucial work of a great Jesuit theologian called Karl Rahner, who wrestled for a long time with the problem of developing a more positive attitude to the non-Christian faiths. It was he who coined the phrase we met a few pages ago, with the concept of the "anonymous Christian". Rahner did not deny the pre-eminent status of Christianity as the witness to the full revealing of God in the person of Jesus Christ. But he believed that Christianity witnessed to a God who would stop at nothing to reveal the truth to his creation – he believed that God has chosen to reach people through the medium of other faiths and movements as well as

Christianity. God may choose to enter into the life of the believer through the devotion of a Hindu at prayer or the ecstatic experience of a Sufi mystic. God has a will to reveal himself to people in ways that are not limited to Christianity, and these ways include other religious systems and traditions.

This conviction, Rahner recognized, has profound implications for the way Christians approach those of other faiths. They should not be seen as ignorant, or blind, or as enemies of the truth. They should be recognized as people who are responding in their own way to the generosity of God. They should be seen as people who are being transformed by the saving power of Jesus Christ, which by the generosity of God is available way out beyond the boundaries of Christianity. They should be seen in fact as Christians who do not know that they are following Christ – as "anonymous Christians".

This view has a lot of virtues, and appeals to many Christians who are unhappy with the flavor of the other views we have examined so far. Above all it recognizes the strength of traditional Christian teaching about the greatness and the power of God, and the desire of God to give humanity every chance. It recognizes that God is greater than the Church, and that God cannot be tied down to work-ing only within the bounds of one human organization. Not only does he reveal himself decisively in the life of one man in a remote Eastern province of the first-century Roman empire, but he also has the generosity to reveal himself in many and various ways to many and various people. This is a powerful view, drawing on the insights of the old Logos theology and tracking back to that inspired linking of ideas in the prologue to the Gospel of John.

It gives Christians a reason to be a great deal more positive about the beliefs, customs and traditions of their non-Christian neigh-bors. It means that those elements of other faiths which seem to be in tune with Christianity can be recognized as being rooted in contact with the same God. There is a certain generosity of spirit here, rather than what seems to be a rather mean-spirited denial of the value of anything that is not Christian. Similarly there is a hu-mility about this approach, and humility is something that we could often do with more of. There are answers, this view says, which lie outside our borders. We do not have it all sewn up. God works in other ways too.

All this is true; and I have found that this inclusivist view often commends itself to those Christians who wish to develop an attitude that is not condemnatory or hostile to other faiths, and who wish to recognize all that is of God in the traditions of others. So far so good. But you will notice that so far we have been looking at the advantages of this view from – as it were – an in-house perspective. We have been saying it gives the Christian a better attitude to people of other faiths. We have been getting dangerously close to patting ourselves on the back and saying "Haven't we done well to develop this positive and inclusive view?"

Let's just try to flip it over and think of it another way. Let us suppose that some positive and inclusive Sikh writer noted the similarity between some of the ethics and some of the theology of the Sikh faith and that of Christianity, realized there was a lot of common ground, and developed the theory that Christians were in fact "anonymous Sikhs". How would we like that? I think many of us would not be very happy at someone from outside our faith telling us that he knew more about us than we did ourselves. We might be tempted to respond along these lines: "What gives you the right to tell us we are not who we think we are? What gives you the right to tell us that we are actually like you, only we don't know it? We do not want to be labeled as anonymous versions of you – we know who we are, we are Christians, we are proud of it, and we don't believe we need re-defining!"

And once we have seen it from that point of view, from outside rather than from inside the comfortable Christian club, it does not seem quite so attractive. In this view of relations with other faiths, Christians are no longer claiming the religious high ground in order to condemn or to judge – and that is certainly a welcome move. But in fact Christians who think like this are still claiming the right to tell other people who they are and how they relate to us. It's a more friendly message; but it still comes from a position of claimed superiority. Some people who do not like this view even talk about arrogance and about condescension. And here is a problem. Rahner himself recognized this: he said that "anonymous Christian" was not a label to be imposed on those outside Christianity, but a helpful way for Christians to think among themselves about those of other faiths. Certainly this helps; but to use language inside the Church about other people, which feels offensive to them when they hear it, is somehow not a very satisfactory way of carrying on.

Undeniably inclusivism is an attractive view. It challenges Christians to treat other faiths with respect and reverence, and to remember that God is a good deal greater than Christianity, and may deal with others in ways which we can neither imagine nor understand, appropriate to wildly different cultures and ways of thinking. But there are elements which some find unsatisfactory – above all the fact that this view claims to know more about other faiths than they know about themselves. Like all the other views which start "We're right", and then go on to say something about "you", this is a view which uses Christianity as the yardstick or standard by which to judge all else. It says nicer things about the other faiths than the previous views we have looked at; but it still says them from a superior point of view, and this is still not a wholly satisfactory position from which to move forward together. So it may still be worth trying to find another way of looking at things, while acknowledging all the virtues of this one.

5

We are right and so are you – so that's all right then!

This one certainly gets away from Christians sitting in judgment on others and telling them that they are wrong, or only partly right, or that they might be members of the club without even knowing it. I've chosen a slightly provocative chapter title, and it is not really fair to some of the scholars I am going to mention, so I shall have to be very careful later on in this chapter! But I have chosen it because there are a number of ways of looking at the relationship between faiths which come under the general heading of "pluralism", and this is a reasonable way of summing up the popular understanding of pluralism. It is an attractive and popular option for many Christians who have become dissatisfied with the previously discussed positions, and it has been the subject of a huge amount of writing in the last twenty-five years. It has certainly influenced me a lot, but I don't want this popular understanding of pluralism to be the last word of this book (as you'll gather from the fact you are still less than half way through!). So let's have a closer look.

I first met and discussed it while I was a graduate student at Oxford University, but it was not in an academic context at all. It was in a book which was being studied in fellowship groups at the Wesley Memorial Methodist Church, which my wife and I attended at the time. The book was associated with a series of BBC radio programs entitled "Priestland's Progress", in which the BBC's Religious Affairs correspondent interviewed many well known Christian figures, and it was billed as "one man's attempt to discover if he is really a Christian". It was an unusually open-minded choice for a fellowship group, and it was valuable for two reasons. First, it made available some insight into the thinking of a wide range of Christian figures, and highlighted the rich variety of thinking and understanding that exists even within the bounds of the mainstream denominations. Second, it made clear to me, and to other members of the group, that ordinary Christians could work things out for themselves. In the conservative evangelical world of my upbringing, the emphasis had been much more upon accepting the authority of the leader, and taking on board the leader's interpretation of Scripture. Here was an eye-opener – the ordinary Christian looking at a range of options and really thinking about developing his understanding. At the same time I was beginning to study the theology of the early Church, and discovering that the early Christians, from the New Testament writers onwards, were going through a similar process of trying to work out how best to understand and express their faith. And here, in the urbane, intelligent, and down-to-earth work of Gerald Priestland, was a modern Christian trying to do exactly the same. It's not a great book; but it was one of those formative influences that came at the right time and in the right place for me. Ever since, in my ministry as a clergyman of the Church of England, and as a teacher of theology and philosophy at university and high school level, I have encouraged students to work things out for themselves, using all the information and insights available. This book has the same objective: work out where you stand!

Anyway, back to Priestland. When he tackles the question of other faiths, he does not do so particularly systematically. He gives a fair crack of the whip to a range of opinions, exclusive and inclusive, before embarking on what he calls "something of a purple passage" and developing an image which is probably familiar to many of us. He uses the metaphor of a mountain, to try to help us see how different faiths might relate to one another. The mountain is God: vast, the summit hidden in mist and the limits stretching further than the eye can see. Different groups see it from different viewpoints, emphasize different aspects of it, and develop different routes up it. The routes are equally valid, though different, just as the views of the mountain are equally valid, though different:

> "It is all the same mountain, seen from different angles; and to deny any of these points of view is to diminish the true nature of the mountain. ... We can all witness together to the existence, majesty and glory of the mountain."

In seeking a route up the mountain, we will naturally follow a guide whom we trust; but we should not be surprised or worried if others, from different starting-points, choose different guides and develop different routes.

> "How futile it is to criticize each other for not having arrived on precisely the same path together! We cannot turn back (though some are tempted to). We can only do our best from where we are. But we are still on the same mountain." **(All quotations are from Priestland G, Priestland's Progress, London, 1981, p 101.)**

This vision of the different faiths as different routes up the same mountain is one which is attractive and appealing to Christians who react against exclusivism and find inclusivism rather condescending. It enables them to be positive about the value of every faith, and to emphasize common ground and a shared enterprise, yet also to be faithful to their own tradition. They can say quite happily that they find Christianity the best route for them, given their starting-point, without showing any disrespect or passing any judgment on those who have started on a different route. They can even agree that individuals may have compelling reasons for changing routes from time to time, or starting a new path, without that implying a value-judgment that anyone else should share. And finally they can agree that the mountain is a far more exciting place with all these routes upon it, than it would be with just one. The mountain is bigger than any one route; it can accommodate all of them.

This can be a liberating vision for those who see real value in different traditions, and do not want to appear to be seeing them and judging them from a superior point of view. There are problems with it, of course, and we shall get to them later in the chapter: but for now, let's have a look at the more academic side of the pluralist way of thinking. This arises out of an awareness that the world has changed since the time when different faiths had their own place and their own agenda, and had little opportunity and little need to work alongside each other or develop a common approach to the challenge of living together. It is a commonplace to say that we now live in a "global village" where ease of travel and communication and cultural interchange has meant that we need to relate to each other in new and different ways.

Many theologians in the recent past have looked at these changes in the world, and have argued that theology is going through a corresponding change. They have started talking about a "paradigm shift". This is an expression borrowed from the history of science, and drawing on the work of Thomas Kuhn in his ground-breaking work "The Structure of Scientific Revolutions". It refers to the point when new evidence becomes so strong that it forces scientists to question certain assumptions that they have previously taken for granted. This keeps on happening: in the twentieth century, since the era of Max Planck, Niels Bohr and Albert Einstein, quantum physics has been bringing about one such paradigm shift; science has been obliged to move on from the security of Newtonian physics, and to accept that the way the world should be viewed has changed for ever. A paradigm shift is bound to happen now and again, as science responds to new investigations and new discoveries and new ideas. Without such shifts, understanding would not develop: it would stagnate and become irrelevant.

Theologians who talk in these terms say that in the world of theology, too, a paradigm shift has become necessary, and indeed is in the process of happening. They say that what we now know and understand about the diverse faiths of humanity cannot any longer be adequately expressed within the old exclusivist and inclusivist theories. They say that we need to shift to a new way of seeing things – a new theology of religions that will better express the way we now experience things. This idea first came into my orbit in a developed form in 1983, when the British SCM Press published a book by Alan Race called "Christians and Religious Pluralism". Here I found for the first time a clear explanation of the three positions of exclusivism, inclusivism, and pluralism, and a development in academic terms of the popular view I had met in Priestland.

Since then I have come to associate the position most strongly with the philosopher of religion John Hick. He has become associated with one particular way of talking about paradigm shifts, as he argues for a "Copernican Revolution" in Christian attitudes towards other faiths. The insights of Copernicus in the sixteenth century revolutionized the previous understanding of our solar system. Previously, the Ptolemaic view of the universe was taken for granted, in which the Earth was placed at the center of the universe. After Copernicus this view had to be changed, and it was now recognized that the Sun was at the center of the solar system, and the Earth moved around it together with the other planets. The paradigm shift had displaced the earth from the center of the universe. Hick has argued eloquently that a parallel "Copernican revolution" is needed in the way we view the relationships between faiths. No longer should Christianity be seen as the central point round which all else revolves, and by reference to which all else is judged. Instead God, or what he later calls the Real, should be give the central place, and Christianity and the other faiths become the planets circling around God, each in their own particular orbit but all deriving their course from God. Christianity ceases to be at the center, as it always has been (at least in its own estimation!) and becomes one among many. The many are equally valid and equally authentic ways of relating to God.

But are they equally true? Hick tends to say so. In "The Rainbow of Faiths" (1995, p 26f), he explains his understanding helpfully by using the analogy of maps. The three-dimensional globe can be represented on two-dimensional flat maps in a variety of ways, using a variety of different projections. They will look very different; and if you compare one with another it would be very easy to jump to the conclusion that one was right and another was wrong. But in fact, providing they are properly drawn, each is equally accurate. It would be very confusing to use two maps with different projections at the same time, and it would be wrong to find one projection lacking because it did not conform to the conventions of another. Each is equally accurate, although they look very different. Hick suggests the theologies of the different religions are like maps with different projections, each trying to represent the complexity of God within the conventions of human thought – a much more difficult task than merely reducing three dimensions to two! And he explains:

> "It could be that the conceptual maps drawn by the great traditions, although finite picturings of the Infinite, are all more or less equally reliable within their different projections, and more or less equally useful for guiding us on our journey through life."

Obviously the map that is most useful to us is the map with whose conventions we are most familiar, but according to Hick we can quite cheerfully allow others to use their own maps, in the confidence that they are as reliable as ours, even if they look very different.

This is a very helpful analogy, to explain how Hick can recognize the differences between religions, but still maintain that they are all responses to the same God, or Reality. But is it quite good enough? There are two different angles from which some people will want to object to this. First, there are those who will want to claim that in fact there is only one projection which is valid and therefore only one map which is accurate. This takes us back to the exclusivist viewpoint, and we must remember all the time that the views we have already examined are held by many Christians. I have in front of me a little book called "Questions and Answers from the Bible" by the evangelist Roger Carswell. Dealing with the question of the truth-claims of other faiths, Carswell suggests that deciding what to believe is not like choosing your ten favorite songs, where there is a subjective element, and what is the right answer for you might be different for someone else. He says it is like guessing the number of peas in a jar: one answer is right and all the others are wrong. One faith is true and all the others are false. Asked a little later in the book to justify this, in answer to the question: "Do all religions lead to God?", Carswell quotes John 14.6 ("I am the way, the truth, and the life. No one comes to the Father except through me.") and Acts 4.12 ("Neither is there salvation in any other, for there is no other name under heaven given among men by which we must be saved."), and sums up the matter by a bit of straight talking: "...if Jesus is right then all the other religions are wrong! Right?" (Carswell, 1996, p 26f)

Well, this reminds us how far pluralism is from the traditional exclusivist view from which we started, and which Carswell represents. Hick would say things are less simple than guessing the number of peas in a jar. He would remind us that two people can look at the same thing and see it very differently: he uses a famous philosophical example of a drawing which can look like both a duck and a rabbit, so that some people can say it is a duck, and some can say it is a rabbit. One can imagine all sorts of arguments about this, especially between people who are familiar with rabbits and not ducks, or vice versa. Both sides would be firmly convinced that they are right. The interesting thing is that both groups are right; but neither group is justified in saying that the other is wrong, even though the other group is saying something very different. In fact both are right. Hick will also remind us, drawing on the philosopher Kant, that when we look at something we use everything we already know to make sense of what we see. We fit what we see into the categories with which we are already familiar. To give a well-known Biblical example, there is an account in Mark chapter nine of Jesus healing a boy whose symptoms included falling to the ground, rolling around, going stiff, and foaming at the mouth. When the first-century people of Judaea looked at the boy, they applied their understanding of the world to him and viewed him as being possessed by an evil spirit. When we twenty-first century people read that story, with our experience of modern medical science, we read the list of symptoms, apply our understanding of the world, and view him as an epileptic. We see the world in different ways. Perhaps too, we see

God in different ways, according to our tradition and culture and faith, and like the duck party and the rabbit party, we do not have the right to say that people who see things differently are wrong.

Here are two very different ways of looking at truth. One group claims to have it pinned down. Another claims that truth is much greater and more complex than our limited attempts to understand and express it, and that there is value in more than one way of trying to express it. We must decide where we stand – but before we do so, we should at least do our best to understand why others might see things differently.

Returning to Hick and the maps, there is another angle from which objection comes, and it is completely different from the last one. People who come from this angle will say to Hick: "Yes, that is a nice job. We recognize your motives and applaud them. We see that you want to acknowledge all that is good in all faiths, and recognize the deep devotion to God and the saintliness and the deep spiritual life which you perceive in your friends from other faiths. That is all great. But have you not gone a bit far? Are you not a bit too ready to accept the truth of all truth-claims? Have you not been a bit too quick to abandon the possibility that some teaching in some religions might actually be wrong, and that some religious ways of life might be less good than others?"

We could return to the maps analogy to clarify this point. Look back – we said that *providing they are properly drawn*, each is equally accurate. It stands to reason that if we want to check that a map is accurate, we should satisfy ourselves that it is properly drawn. In the case of maps, for the professional cartographer, this is not too hard, with accurate measurements and tools, and satellite pictures, and so forth. It is a necessary check. But in the case of religions it is not quite as easy. Is Hick is a bit too ready to accept that all the theological projections are properly drawn? He does not talk about checking this out at all.

And yet when we look closer, it does not quite seem so obvious that all religious ways of life are equally true representations of a life lived in harmony with God. Those faiths for instance which demand the sacrifice of a human being to expiate sin or appease an angry god are not quite on a par with the Buddhist way of peace or the non-violence of the Hindu tradition of Gandhi. This seems self-evident: yet has Hick abandoned the right to make that judgment, by pleading that each of us sees God through the mental spectacles of our own culture and understanding? Is there a danger that plural-ism, in its desire to affirm the value in every faith, becomes unable to make critical judgments? Is it just a matter of "anything goes"?

This easy acceptance of every religious way cannot be accepted as smoothly as this. The maps are in fact very different indeed. They may be maps of one life followed by judgment, or of many lives governed by the unchanging law of karma. They may be maps of a personal God, or an impersonal God, or of no God at all in the case of Buddhist traditions. They may define evil as rebellion against God, or simply make evil part of the pattern of life, with a God whose nature encompasses both good and evil. Hick would deal with this by reminding us that these different views arise from limited human perspectives on Reality which is greater and more complex than any of them; but we must at the very least remain aware that there are enormous differences between religious faiths and ways of life, and we should not play them down by just stress-ing the similarities. The paths up the mountain are very different indeed, and it is facile to think otherwise. In fact you could easily argue that they are not even climbing the same mountain!

And here of course we need to do more thinking about the mountain analogy. At the start of the chapter we accepted the at-tractive image of different paths up the mountain without critique. But in fact there are certain important assumptions lurking within it. For a start, we are assuming quite happily that there is only one mountain. Of course that seems natural to people from a Christian background: we are used to taking it for granted that there is only one God, and moreover we are used to sharing our God with Judaism. Some of us believe we are sharing our God with Islam too: others don't. And where does the very different view of the divine in Hindu traditions fit in? It may be an attractive thought to suggest that we are all making our way up the same mountain, but it is an assumption.

And even if we are, anyone who has done any hill-walking will know that paths can be deceptive. They may look as if they are going the same way, but they don't always. Some are made by sheep and lead you to places where sheep can go but people can't. Some are more dangerous and treacherous than others. Some may fade out part-way in a bog and leave you floundering around knee-deep in mud (seems to happen to me a lot!). I could develop this further, but the point is made. Not every path is as good as the next one. It is not good enough to suggest that they will all get there in the end. We could only know that if we were hovering above the summit of the mountain in a helicopter taking aerial photographs, and we cannot do that in the case of the God mountain!

So maybe there are different summits or even different mountains! And maybe some of the paths are actually better than others. The problem here arises from the pluralist view of the religious universe, following Hick's "Copernican revolution". In the old view, with Christianity at the center, it used to be easy to judge everything else by reference to Christianity. We have noted already that there are problems with sitting in judgment on others from a position of superiority; but at least it was clear what was going on! In Hick's revolutionized religious view, God is at the center. That's fine of course; but we cannot judge from God's point of view. We have no helicopter hovering over the mountain. We have lost our frame of reference. We can't make judgments about the different paths. That may be good in that it means we are not negative about our friends who follow other traditions, and we are a bit less inclined to be smug ourselves; but it also means that we have a real problem deciding what is a good and helpful element in any tradition, and what is not.

There tends to be a kind of assumption lurking in the pluralist camp that we can actually be in the position of the helicopter: that we have the full picture and can say with confidence that every path will reach the same summit. We need to be clear that this is not the case. Hick, to be fair, would agree. He says that this way of looking at things is a "hypothesis" – that is, a theory constructed to fit all the evidence as well as possible. It is better, he says, than the old hypothesis which placed Christianity at the center, but he accepts that it is a theory which may need to be modified in the light of further evidence or further thinking. That is a fair and honest statement of where he stands. He has developed a view which he believes is a "best fit" to the evidence; but it may need to be modifies in the light of further understanding. It is a hypothesis; it is *provisional*. This is a key point, and we shall return to it.

Some pluralists have attempted to go a stage further, and develop some way of saying which kind of path is better. These tend to focus on the outcomes of particular way of believing and living – a kind of application of the "By their fruits you shall know them" principle to which we referred back in chapter 2. Another key player alongside Hick in the development of pluralism, Paul Knitter, is now working with ideas taken from liberation theology to argue that we can judge the authenticity of a faith by its liberating effects. At the risk of over-simplifying, if a religious tradition serves to liberate the oppressed and correct injustice, then it is good; if it doesn't, it isn't. This is fairly close to the gut-reaction by which we agreed a few pages ago that faiths which encouraged human sacrifice were on the whole not as good as faiths that don't. Others adopt a similar line in suggesting that we should try to pull out the best insights of religious and philosophical traditions to construct a "global ethic", and then use that as a yardstick to judge the faiths and their effects.

These seem to be promising developments, even taking into account the difficulty of agreeing on a global ethic, and the problem which arises when liberation is achieved by questionable means. But there is a lurking problem: all of this is about the effects of a faith in practical living, and here the mainstream faiths are generally in reasonably close harmony. Pluralists of course emphasize this. But does the fact that you have your ethics reasonably well sorted out actually mean that your theology is good?

Perhaps we can find a way forward by using the kind of critical judgment that we are used to seeing within faith traditions. All of us are used to seeing key principles of our faith used in a process of internal critique. It is generally agreed among Christians, for instance, that too often in our history, Christians have not dealt appropriately with those who disagree with them. The Spanish Inquisition is often cited as a case in point, and so are the Crusades. The Inquisition was a vicious campaign ruthlessly to suppress heresy within the Christian Church, and the crusades were an equally vicious campaign to remove the "infidel" from the holy places of early Christian history. There are many other examples, none of which really fit in with the overall thrust of – for instance – the Great Commandment to love God and our neighbor (Mark 12.30–31). The critique proceeds here by taking a central principle of the faith, and using it to raise questions about particular incidents in Christian history which do not seem to honor that principle. More controversially, the same can be done with reference to the contemporary Church. It is not easy, though, and much depends on what key principle is chosen. For instance, Christians who like myself try to take a lead from the Great Commandment will perhaps have a different view in current arguments about gay clergy and female Bishops from those who base their position on Biblical inerrancy and certain key texts.

Nevertheless, judgments of that kind can be made in self-critique within a faith position. Many Muslim leaders are currently involved in making that kind of judgment about violence and terrorism, arguing that the actions and principles of the 9/11 or 7/7 terrorists arise from a fatal distortion of Islam, and that such violence has no place or sanction within Islam. By a process of internal critique based on understanding the central teaching of their faith, they seek to purify their tradition and distance themselves from those who do evil in the name of Islam.

These judgments, though, are all internal matters, like discussions conducted within a family on principles agreed within the family. We all tend to use principles from deep within our own faith and tradition to reach decisions on what is and is not right. I have indicated my own tendency to rest on the Great Commandment of Mark 12.28–34. In the discussion reported here, Jesus and a scholar of the Jewish Law reached agreement on the question of which commandment was the greatest of all. Jesus drew on Jewish tradition to put together two separate elements of the Jewish Law, from Deuteronomy and Exodus, in one powerful pairing:

"Love the Lord your God with all your heart, with all your
soul, with all your mind, and with all your strength, ...
Love your neighbor as yourself."

When the scholar not only agreed, but also commented that "It is
more important to obey these two commandments than to offer
animals and other sacrifices to God", he was told by Jesus "You are
not far from the Kingdom of God". This teaching gives simple and
powerful guidance to Christians, and is close to the ethic of other
major faiths. As far as I am concerned, those who act out of devotion to God (however understood) and love of their neighbor are
doing fine.

Now as a rule of thumb, that serves me well, and I commend
it for practical use. But note what I am doing here. I am taking a
principle deeply entrenched in my own heritage, in the teaching of
Jesus and the tradition of Christianity, and I am using it to make
judgments about others. On its basis I can develop positive attitudes
to many followers of other faiths than mine; and sadly I can also
use it to raise serious concerns about some fellow members of my
own faith. I am using the Great Commandment in the kind of way
Knitter might use the principle of liberation. But are we really being
pluralist here? I have to say not. We are using principles from our
own tradition to make a generous judgment about others. Isn't this
inclusivism? It is not any longer the "We are right and so are you"
position. It is more a case of "We are right and so are we all – *to the
extent that* we are all in harmony with the Great Commandment".
We have found our yardstick to help us make informed judgments;
but it is a yardstick from our own tradition. We have gone back to
a generous kind of inclusivism, but nevertheless it is no more than
inclusivism. It is on our terms, not on equal terms.

And so we are forced – so far! – to two interim conclusions. First,
true pluralism is founded upon the assumption that religious traditions are basically working in the same direction, and that their
claims to truth are equally valid. Second, if we question this assumption, and try to find grounds for making decisions about those
truth-claims, we are driven back to using criteria from within our

own traditions, and therefore back to inclusivism. And yet we found there were problems with inclusivism, and they haven't gone away in the meantime.

So where do we go from here? We have looked in detail at all the standard ways of working out how the truth-claims of different religious traditions relate to each other, and we have found significant problems with all of them. If we are to move forward, we are going to have to examine how exactly these truth-claims have developed, and what exactly is going on in the formation of religious traditions. We shall come to this in chapter seven. But first, we should consider an increasingly popular alternative response to this problem of the relationship between faiths, just to ensure that we have covered all possible bases.

6

We are all completely wrong except the atheists

Another provocative title, this one, but it represents a position which we must acknowledge and consider, and this seems the sensible time to do so. If we cannot find a satisfactory way of understanding how different ways of believing in God relate to each other, perhaps that indicates that there is a fundamental problem with believing in God at all. Perhaps we should have the courage to admit that this whole business of believing in God is a castle built on shifting foundations, and abandon the whole business as a bad job. That is the position adopted by a number of increasingly vocal advocates of atheism, and it is taken up with enthusiasm by those who can see that there are many problems with religious traditions. Indeed some of these problems have been at the heart of our discussions so far: if believers maintain that they are right and all others are wrong, they can become aggressive, militant, and judgmental of others, and if they regard everyone as equally right, they can become uncritical and undiscriminating, and fail to offer any clear lead or distinctive insight into the human condition. So if the outcomes of religion are either negative or woolly-minded, why not abandon the whole thing as a bad job and get rid of all this superstitious nonsense about divine beings?

Certainly this adoption of atheism appears to sidestep an awful lot of problems at a single stroke, and this kind of radical approach to problem-solving is always attractive. It is a bit like the story told by Plutarch of Alexander the Great and the Gordian Knot. It seems that during Alexander's campaigns in Asia Minor in 333 BC, the Macedonian king adopted an original approach to a challenge which had defeated many cunning men before him. In the city of Gordium was an ancient chariot, secured to its yoke by an intricate and complicated knot; the local legend was that any man who could untie it was destined to become the ruler of the world. The ends were invisible and no-one had ever been able to untie the knot; but Alexander adopted the radical solution of slashing it through with his sword, separated the chariot from its yoke, and in due course went on to become the ruler of pretty much the entire known world. It was a simple solution, it got rid of the problem, and of course in practical terms it achieved the desired effect: it established Alexander's authority in the area and enhanced his reputation (though the backing of a Greek war-host under his command can't have done any harm either!).

Some of the atheist scholars who argue for the rejection of religion, such as Professor Richard Dawkins of Oxford University, like to present themselves in a similar fashion, as practical men who can cut through the tangled knots of superstition and groundless belief, and enhance their reputation for clear no-nonsense thinking. And theirs is an approach which has a great deal of appeal in a world which values rational thinking and evidence-based science. But we must ask, is the matter quite that simple? After all, this is not just a matter of finding a practical solution to a practical problem, like untying a knot; it is a matter of trying to work out what people should believe about God, and how people with different beliefs about God should relate to one another. It may be the most important question in the world, and it is important to try to get it right. So in considering the attractions of the atheist option, we must ask three questions. We must ask whether this option does in fact sidestep the problems quite as effectively as it initially seems to; we must ask whether it is as simple a solution as it appears; and of course we must ask whether it is actually likely to be right?

The atheist option is often presented as the rational alternative to the irrational superstition that is belief in God. There are many different religious traditions, we are told, with different and often conflicting ideas about God, or gods. They range from animism to polytheism to monotheism; they cannot possibly all be right, and so most probably are all wrong. Even if you go for one of these – let's say Christianity – its teachings are contradictory and probably nonsensical, and moreover they are morally and ethically objectionable. If you want examples of contradiction, consider the problem of believing in a God who is supposed to exemplify justice and love, and yet tells lies to his first creations in the first chapter of Genesis, almost destroys his creation in the flood episode in the seventh, and turns Lot's wife into a pillar of salt in the nineteenth because she looks back at her home which he has just destroyed. Or, to be slightly more controversial, promises a land to his chosen people which already belongs to someone else. That one is still causing huge problems in the Middle East to this day. If you want nonsensical, consider the doctrine of the Trinity, which splits the one God of the Judaeo-Christian tradition into three persons, Father, Son, and Holy Spirit, who yet comprise only one God. However many convenient words like "triune" are coined in the theological tradition, it is very hard to maintain that one equals three equals one without looking a bit silly to those outside the tradition. This is one of the things which prevent many Muslims from seeing Christianity as a monotheistic faith. And if you want morally objectionable, try the doctrine of substitutionary atonement: the idea that God requires humanity to undergo punishment for sin, but is quite happy to transfer the entire punishment to his innocent Son.

I could go on and on – but this is quite enough to give a flavor of the happy time that militant opponents of religion can have, ridiculing some of the more unfortunate features of religious tradition. It is not hard, and it is undoubtedly fun. My high school students love playing this game. But please note exactly what game it is. It is a game which points out some of the strange ideas which human beings have developed about God. It is a game which ridicules some of the more bizarre features of religious traditions developed by human beings. It is a game, really, which points out that people can believe some very strange and very silly and very unpleasant things. Where is the surprise there? Of course they can. Many people believe in morally objectionable political systems, and many people believe that little gray beings from another planet abduct humans in flying saucers. That does not mean that humans are wrong to engage in politics, and it does not mean that there are not necessarily other sentient beings in this vast and wondrous universe. Equally, the fact that some people believe some rather odd things about God does not necessarily mean that belief in God is itself odd, or wrong.

You see what is going on here? The opponents of religion are confusing religion with belief in God. They may have shown that there are some rather strange things about religious traditions; that is a fair point, and we shall have to deal with it in the next chapter. But they have not managed to show, just by ridiculing some features of religion, that there is anything wrong at all with believing in God.

Yet they decide, because they can show that some religious beliefs are rather strange, to opt instead for what they present as the rational alternative. Much better, they say, to believe in no God. To believe that there is no God at all. This rational position is much better than the irrationality of a multitude of irrational and irreconcilable faith positions. This sidesteps all the problems posed by the religious traditions.

But does it? It would, certainly, if it were indeed wholly rational, or if it could be proved. It would be a proven position that would do away with the need for all the religious speculation, all the religious beliefs and ideas. But let us be clear what kind of statement they are making. They are not saying "I do not believe in God" – that is, they are not simply refusing to make a statement that goes beyond the evidence and rests on faith. To refuse to make such a statement would be rational. But the atheists are going beyond the rational – they are saying "I believe that there is no God", and that is an equal and opposite faith-statement to the theist one. It too goes beyond the evidence and rests on faith.

This is a crucial point. The atheist position is a position of faith. It looks at the evidence presented in the world, and on the basis of that evidence, and of certain assumptions, proceeds beyond that evidence to a faith-statement that there is no divine being. It is exactly parallel to the position which looks at the evidence presented in the world, and on the basis of that evidence, and of certain assumptions, proceeds beyond that evidence to a faith-statement that there is a divine being. The atheist position is, in terms of rationality, no better and no worse than the theist. The evidence is ambiguous: it can be interpreted in theist or atheist terms. The assumptions which lead theists and atheists to interpret the evidence differently need examining, of course; if one group's assumptions are clearly more sensible than the other's, then there will be some ground for making a decision between them. We shall have a look at them soon. But in the meantime, the two positions must be treated as equal and opposite. The atheist position has not sidestepped the problems: in fact it has added to them, by presenting yet another interpretation of reality, which must be taken into account alongside all the other interpretations provided by religious faith. We can now add atheistic faith to the complicated picture.

Just to be completely clear, if you want a purely rational position, which does not go beyond the evidence, it will be the position of reserved judgment known as agnosticism. I am well acquainted with this position. It was that adopted by my father, who was an eminent research metallurgist, a Fellow of the New York Academy of Sciences, and a Fellow of the Royal Society, which elects the most eminent scholars of each scientific generation in Britain to its membership. He believed in examining evidence, and constructing justifiable hypotheses and theories on the basis of it, but he did not regard the evidence for or against God as sufficiently strong to justify constructing any theory. He therefore adopted the purely rational position of agnosticism. He had read T H Huxley as a young man, and remained persuaded by the intellectual position for which Huxley coined the term "agnostic", as related in this extract:

> "When I reached intellectual maturity, and began to ask
> myself whether I was an atheist, a theist, or a pantheist;
> a materialist or an idealist; a Christian or a freethinker,

I found that the more I learned and reflected, the less ready was the answer; until at last I came to the conclusion that I had neither art nor part with any of these denominations, except the last. The one thing in which most of these good people were agreed was the one thing in which I differed from them. They were quite sure that they had attained a certain 'gnosis' – had more or less successfully solved the problem of existence; while I was quite sure I had not, and had a pretty strong conviction that the problem was insoluble. And, with Hume and Kant on my side, I could not think myself presumptuous in holding fast by that opinion.

"So I took thought, and invented what I conceived to be the appropriate title of 'agnostic'. It came into my head as suggestively antithetic to the 'gnostic' of Church history, who professed to know so much about the very things of which I was ignorant; and I took the earliest opportunity of parading it at our Society, to show that I, too, had a tail, like the other foxes." (Huxley, T H, "Agnosticism", in *The Nineteenth Century*, February, 1889.)

At the same time, John Stuart Mill was stating that "The rational attitude of a thinking mind toward the supernatural, whether in natural or revealed religion, is that of scepticism, as distinguished from belief on one hand and from atheism on the other". (Mill, J S, "Theism", in Essays on Religion, 1874.) These writers were clear, as we should be, that both theism and atheism are faith statements which go beyond the evidence.

Having clarified the rationality of agnosticism, and the equal and opposite status of the faith-statements that there is a God, and that there is not one, we have answered our first question. The atheists have not avoided the problems of the multitude of faith-statements: they have just complicated matters further by adding another one. But we must still ask: is their solution simpler? Is their faith-statement a simple and obvious one which elegantly accounts for all the evidence? Is it more justifiable than the opposite faith-statement of belief in a God? For if it is, we must take it very seriously indeed.

The trouble is, our answer to this question depends on our view of the assumptions which lie behind the faith-statement. The atheist faith depends on the assumption that the material world around us is all that there is. We are seen as no more than physical beings in a physical world; our nature, and the nature of our world and our universe, can be investigated by science and will eventually be fully understood by science. The way of understanding the universe which involves belief in God is seen as a primitive and superstitious misunderstanding, which will eventually be blown out of the water when science has advanced further. The assumption here is that we can arrive at a full understanding of our universe by scientific investigation, and that any question which science cannot answer – such as why the universe is here at all – is a meaningless question. The empiricist philosopher David Hume provides a wonderful summary of this point of view, which I always make a point of quoting to my students, since it sums up so well the assumption that any question which mathematics and science cannot answer is a meaningless question.

Hume was well known for challenging theological arguments by pointing out that they lacked a serious evidence base, and were therefore pointless. If theologians wanted to argue about the creation of the universe by God, Hume would point out that we have no evidence of how or whether universes are made, and that therefore the theological argument was rather lacking in foundation. He summed up his approach at the conclusion of his 'Enquiry Concerning Human Understanding' in a peroration which has come to be known among philosophy students by the title of "Hume's Bonfire". Part of it goes like this:

> "If we take in our hand any volume, let us ask, Does it contain any abstract reasoning concerning quantity and number? No. Does it contain any experimental reasoning, concerning matter of fact or existence? No. Commit it then to the flames: for it can contain nothing but sophistry and illusion." **(Hume D, An Enquiry concerning Human Understanding, 1748.)**

If it is not mathematics, then, and not experimental science, it is nonsense. It is "sophistry and illusion" – false reasoning based on no more than imagination. Any discussion of a divine being, or of the spiritual part of life, or of questions of meaning and purpose, is empty talk, signifying nothing. Now this is all very well, and if you share this kind of assumption, you will find the atheist position simpler and more appealing than the theist. I often sum up this assumption for my students with the tag phrase "What you see is what you get". Many scientists, though not all by any means, share this view.

Others believe that there is more to this world than meets the eye, and that there is perhaps more to this world than science can show. And this is the equivalent tag with which I sum up the religious believer's approach: that there is more to this world than meets the eye. This is, again, an equal and opposite assumption. It amounts to a conviction that what you get is actually more than you can immediately see; that there is more to a human being than a collection of molecules or a genetic structure that is desperate to replicate itself; that such ideals as virtue, justice, and love are more than concepts dreamed up by highly evolved intelligent creatures, but actually reflect something fundamental about the nature of the universe, and the ultimate reality upon which it depends.

Neither approach then is simpler than the other; they just depend upon opposite assumptions, opposite hunches, opposite gut-feelings. The agnostic will take the reasonable approach of refusing to be persuaded by either hunch, because it is no more than a hunch, a gut-feeling about the way things are. But many people will jump one way or the other. Which means we must ask – are there good reasons to jump one way rather than the other? Is there any ground for suggesting that one way may be more likely to be right? Are there better grounds for regarding one belief than the other as justifiable?

And here I think there are good grounds for keeping alive the serious possibility of God. There are three areas which we need to examine here: the huge evidence of religious experience, the vast and enduring consensus that there is indeed more to life than meets the eye, and the new possibilities which are being opened up by contemporary science. Each of these encourages us to keep an open mind and to avoid closing off all but one of the options by choosing atheism. Taken together, they give us ground to claim it is not only justifiable but sensible to believe in a divine being or ultimate reality of some kind. What exactly we should believe about him/her/it is another matter; but these indicators will at least encourage us to keep open the option of believing in God, and to pursue further the question of how those who believe in different ways should relate to each other.

First then, religious experience. This is an area about which I find it hard to write, because I am not one of those people who can say with confidence that they have had a religious experience. I am, as you will have gathered by reading this far, quite a rational person. I tend to think things through rather than to act impulsively, and I tend to be suspicious of the instant emotional reaction. Yet I don't think I am an insensitive person; I have stood on mountaintops and by lake shores, and been bowled over by the beauty and majesty of the world around me. I have stood in the profound darkness of a military training area at dead of night, with no artificial light for miles in any direction, and been filled with wonder at the glory of the night sky full of stars. I have been amazed at the glories of the universe revealed by our telescopic probings into the distance of space. Above all, I have been sandbagged by love for the woman who has been my wife for twenty-eight years and my sweetheart for five years before that, and who has been my best friend since I first knew her. I have been melted with love for our children from the first gaze into their bleary little eyes at the moment of birth. I am not insensitive to awe and wonder and love, and all of these things, and many more, have helped to convince me that there is more to life than meets the eye. Yet I have never heard the voice of God or had a vision of God, and I cannot honestly make any claim to understand what that may be like.

Which makes it all the more important that I take a long hard look at those who do make such claims. Fortunately, that is not so hard to do these days, and I can lean heavily on the work of others to get an overall impression of what kind of evidence we are dealing with. The most systematic contemporary study of religious experience is the continuing work of the Religious Experience Research Centre at the University of Wales, Lampeter. The Centre continues the work of the Oxford Religious Experience Research Unit, founded by Prof Sir Alister Hardy FRS in 1969, to conduct a controlled evidence-based study into reports of religious experience. One of the most surprising fruits of nearly 40 years of research has been the sheer number of people, even in contemporary Western European society, who claim to have had such an experience. As well as collecting and analyzing reports of religious experiences (many of which you can examine if you wish on the public website http://www.lamp.ac.uk/aht/Research/research.html), the Unit conducts opinion polls using the following question: "Have you ever had a spiritual or religious experience, or felt a presence of power, whether you called it God or not, which is different from your everyday life?" The results consistently fall between 25% and 45% positive, no matter what the ethnic, social, cultural, or religious background of the interviewees. This is too large a proportion to ignore or to write off as deluded or mistaken without further investigation.

For many of these people, too, the experience is life-changing. It results in a new way of life, or a new understanding of life, or a new belief or conviction about God. It remains of enduring importance for many years, and means that every aspect of life is seen from a new perspective. Sometimes people speak openly and freely about it; but more often the religious experience is something which is kept quiet or secret, treasured to oneself, and only spoken about in company which is trusted to take seriously something which is of such great personal importance. One of the remarkable features of the Research Unit's findings is the large number of people who have never spoken of their experience until given the opportunity to do so by Unit researchers: often they explain that the experience was so important to them that they were unwilling to have it subjected to questioning, rational analysis, or even ridicule by others.

Yet if they are to be used in a discussion of belief in God, of course accounts of religious experience must be subjected to questioning and rational analysis. In particular, they must face the challenge that they can be explained in purely psychological terms. This is a strong challenge, because it does not deny the reality of the experiences or undermine the sincerity of people's accounts; it simply says that the experiences may be explained in psychological terms, and do not necessarily relate to any divine being at all. This may be true; and yet there are certain features which might be used to argue against this. First, often those who have religious experiences are well balanced, intelligent, and rational people, aware of the ambiguity of the experience, and not easily open to persuasion or suggestion. Second, the result of the experience is in many cases a new insight or a change of lifestyle which goes quite against the previous inclination of the person concerned, yet is maintained consistently over a long term period. This is the case with 'conversion' experiences, which are often unlooked-for and even unwanted, and look far more like response to an external stimulus than to an internal psychological aberration. Third, and perhaps most thought-provoking, if there is a God, how else would that God communicate anyway except through the human psyche? To account for religious experiences in psychological terms does not rule out God being behind the psychological effects. The love of one human being for another can be explained in psychological terms, yet the beloved person is the ultimate cause of the love-response, without whom it could not happen. Logically, God can be the ultimate source of the religious experience, however many psychological explanations are advanced for it.

Indeed, one philosopher, William Alston of Syracuse University, suggests that we may have senses or faculties of which we are not fully aware, which enable us to experience God. Just as some of us can hear better than others, or see more clearly (I don't hear all that well myself, and have worn spectacles from the age of seven), some of us may be more sensitive to experience of the divine than others (maybe I am bit lacking in that area too!). This makes sense, given that we are becoming all too aware of our lack of understanding of the human mind and its potential. The possibility certainly indicates that we should not ignore religious experience or write it off.

It should be seen as one indicator that it may be very sensible and justifiable to believe in a divine being.

It is clearly sensible here to be aware of the wider possibilities, rather than closing off all options but one. This is all the more so, given the way in which a belief in the divine has been so central a feature of human experience in many times and many quite independent cultures. Atheists will use the diversity and variety of religious beliefs to rubbish them all: clearly they cannot all be right, they will say, so the likelihood is that none of them is. But it is possible to put the opposite spin on the argument, and to say that the centrality of religious belief to a range of cultures shows that it must be taken seriously. A huge range of different kinds of people, at different times and with wildly different assumptions about life, from the Inuit of the North to the Australian aboriginal in the South, have been aware that there is more to life than meets the eye, and that there is a divine reality lying behind the transitory day-to-day world. The variety of their responses of course needs to be accounted for – and will be, in the next chapter – but the universality of response to the divine is highly significant. Often there has been a resistance to superstitious and unworthy responses, like that of Socrates in Athens; often there has been a drive to refine and purify a religious tradition, like that of the prophets of Israel; occasionally a radically new response has developed, like that of Christianity or of Islam; but all of these have been a matter of replacing one response to the divine with another one. Up until very recently, it has been pretty much a universal feature of human experience to be aware of the divine and to respond to it in some religious fashion.

So why has it become respectable in our own culture to reserve judgment on the divine, as the agnostic does, or to respond with the faith-statement of atheism, going directly against the accumulated wisdom of previous ages? A full answer would require a book much longer than this one, but a simple answer, fortunately, will answer our needs here. Think back to Hume and his bonfire – he placed his confidence in mathematical and scientific investigation. If math and science couldn't sort out a question, then it wasn't worth sorting. It was just "sophistry and illusion". Huxley and Mill were going the same way: if reasoning, based on evidence and investigation, couldn't give you the answer, then the answer wasn't there. You had to reserve judgment. Their way of thinking is typical of the age in which they lived: an age of increasing confidence in science, and increasing reluctance to accept anything on trust, without evidence. And their age is the direct ancestor of our own. We are taught to trust empirical investigation, to trust experimental science, but not to accept anything else on trust. We are taught to trust the findings of science.

It is fortunate, then, for those of us who believe that there is more to life than meets the eye, that science is increasingly coming around to the same conclusion. Gone for ever is the old nineteenth-century world of Hume, Mill, and Huxley, in which science could have confidence that it was well on the way to understanding everything and answering all questions. Gone for ever is the old world of the physics of Sir Isaac Newton, in which one could be confident that the world was orderly, predictable, and functioned according to laws which we could establish by experiment. During the twentieth century came the absolute revolution of quantum science, and the news has slowly filtered through from the scientific community to the wider world that things are not quite as secure, orderly, or predictable as we thought. Quantum science runs counter to common sense – not surprising, this, since common sense is simply the sum total of our expectations, based on our experience, and quantum science is now telling us that our experience is a pretty poor guide to the way things actually are.

Quantum science seems completely counter-intuitive: for example, according to quantum physics, particles can be in two places at the same time; particles on opposite sides of the universe can affect each other, without there being any connection between them; particles can travel faster than the speed of light; and mutually exclusive states of affairs can exist simultaneously. If you don't believe me, go find out about Schrödinger's cat, which can be understood as being alive and not alive at the same time. This example was originally put forward as an attempt to disprove quantum theory, because it seemed so ridiculous, but oddly enough it turned out not to disprove it at all.

Enough of this. Fortunately for our purposes, we are not called upon to understand quantum theory. All we need to know is that we can no longer assume that the world conforms to early twenty-first century common sense. We can no longer assume that what we see is what we get – not least because in quantum theory the very act of observing something changes it anyway! So what we see is not what we had before we looked! Science has begun to tell us that the world is not orderly, not predictable, not easily to be understood. It has begun to tell us that there are not three or four dimensions, but anything up to twelve, and that we do not understand them at all. It has in fact begun to tell us exactly what believers in God have been saying for a long time – that there is infinitely more to this world than meets the eye, and there is much about it that we do not understand and are indeed only dimly and occasionally aware of. Perhaps religious experience is temporary awareness of this.

Science is learning, in short, not to take a reductionist viewpoint. That is, not to assume that everything can be reduced to ordered patterns and predictable rules. It is learning that the evidence so far established for the way the world works, on the basis of which its theories and hypotheses are formed, is woefully inadequate. It is learning that the universe in which we live is far more complex and mysterious than post-Enlightenment culture has assumed. And it is learning that we have far more questions than answers, far more problems than solutions, and that there is much that we do not and maybe cannot understand. In the light of this, we should be aware that it is wiser to keep an open mind than to limit our options; it is wiser to be alive and open to a wide range of possibilities, than to assume that certain options are closed off just because they do not fit in with our preconceived, simplistic ideas of how things are. And it is arguably wiser and more justifiable, given the complexity of which we are becoming aware, to believe in the existence of an ultimate reality beyond what can be observed – a divine being – rather than to close off the possibility.

So where does this leave us? We have agreed the rationality of the agnostic option, and noted that if we choose to go beyond the strict limits of the ambiguous evidence, there are better grounds for the rich and open-minded option of belief in God than for adopting the reductionist assumptions of atheism. We have, however, become aware that religious traditions have major shortcomings, and huge contradictions, to which atheists are right to draw our attention. We need to account for them and get them into perspective, and we still need to find ways of dealing with their conflicting claims to truth.

So it's back to examining religious traditions. There are two major questions which we need to think about now. We need to decide what exactly religious traditions are. Are they human creations? To what extent do they develop and change? To what extent can we develop or change them further? If you like, are "Copernican revolutions" acceptable in religious matters? And second, we need to ask a closely linked question about Scriptures, if we are to see exactly what force arguments from Scriptural texts have. So let's take a pause, stand back, and have a look at these questions. Then we can go back and see if we can do any more with these vexed questions about who is right and who is wrong.

7

What exactly are religious traditions?

Consider for a moment the origins of Christianity. At a particular time, in a rather troublesome province of the Roman world, a particular human being emerges from obscurity to make a remarkable impact. He develops a reputation for remarkable mighty works, and for controversial actions and challenging teachings. Responses to him vary greatly. To some of his fellow Jews, he is a dangerous radical, a threat to both the political and the religious stability of the region. To others he is a stimulating teacher and a charismatic leader. He appears to some people to be suspiciously cavalier with the Law: he encourages his followers to drop everything and follow him, even to the extent in one case of falling foul of the Fifth Commandment. (To walk out on your father and leave him to run the fishing business on his own, as James and John are reported to have done, is hardly in line with the commandment to "honor your father and mother".) His track record with the Fourth Commandment, about the Sabbath Day, is not too good either. He repeatedly gets into hot water for breaking the Sabbath and encouraging his disciples to do the same. Yet at the same time he seems to many to be a prophet, speaking with authority on behalf of God; and to some he is the promised Messiah, come to set God's people free and re-establish them in their own land under the rule of God and the kingly line of David.

Some people react violently against him; others try to ignore him. And some devote their lives to him. Mark's Gospel, usually regarded as the earliest account, gives us a record of how they gradually worked out their view of him: a charismatic figure with authority which gradually emerged as they accompanied him on his travels. He could heal illness and cast out evil spirits; not too unusual, this, as there were a number of other holy men of the time with similar track records. He could preach on the Scriptures with authority and conviction: this too is not unique, though Mark implies that it was regrettably rare! But he did more than this: he claimed to be able to pronounce forgiveness of sins, which was the prerogative of God, and he was said to do things which should only be possible by the direct power of the creator God. He could control the wind and the waves, they said; he could even raise the dead. They came to believe that he was the Messiah sent by God to the Jewish people; and gradually they came to realize that he was not quite the Messiah they expected, and he was not going to do the things popularly expected of the Messiah. Some came in the end to believe that he was more than the Messiah. They came to believe that when they encountered Jesus, the son of Mary, in the villages and towns of Judaea, they were encountering God as they had never done before. Face to face, they were encountering the power and the authority and the challenges and the demands of God. This was confirmed by the reports of his resurrection, and above all by the experience of the Twelve at Pentecost. They were huddling, disappointed and demoralized, in an obscure meeting-place, when their experience transformed them into the nucleus of a new movement, fuelled with the conviction that they were themselves filled with the same power that they had encountered in Jesus. Filled with that power – that Spirit – they went out and began to change the world.

And as they went out, they and their companions began to try and make sense of their experience. They believed that they had had a unique encounter with God. How were they to explain it? How could they put it into words that others would understand? They had of course some tools to help them. They had the religious tradition of the people of Israel; they had the prophets, and they found in them much which could be applied to Jesus, and which helped them make sense of him. Some had training in the scholarship of the Law and of the Scriptures: Paul, for instance, after he came on the scene, developed an understanding of Jesus as the second Adam, putting right what had gone wrong at the fall which was documented in the book of Genesis. Others as we have seen had their Greek education to help them: John used Greek ideas alongside Hebrew ones to put together the ideas that we examined in chapter four, when we looked at the Prologue to his Gospel.

And they had their experience and their convictions, which demanded new ways of talking about God. They were convinced that in Jesus they had met God; they were convinced that the power of God had changed them at Pentecost. They had ideas of Sonship to wrestle with; and they came up with the radical new ideas of the Incarnation and of the Trinity to explain how God could be the Creator of the world, and be made physical in Jesus as a human being, and be present as the power that inspired the followers of Jesus after his death. John developed the idea of the Logos which was Jesus and yet more than Jesus.

And then the Church argued for four hundred years, and to a considerable extent is arguing still, as to how these things could be expressed in ways that made sense. How did Incarnation work? Was Jesus more divine than human or more human than divine? Or fully divine and fully human? And how could two natures in one person work? Come to that, how could three persons in one God work? What was the rank order among the three persons of the Trinity or were they all equal? Did the Spirit relate equally to the Father and the Son, or were the Son and the Spirit equally subservient to the Father? The Orthodox and Catholic Churches parted company over that one, over a thousand years later, in the Great Schism.

There are two things going on here, and one follows on from the other. First comes the experience, which has a huge effect on the lives of the followers of Jesus. It is for them a definitive encounter with God. Second comes the attempt to make sense of this encounter, using the ideas and the language and the concepts which come to hand, and even fashioning new concepts and new ways of thinking. It is important in thinking about religious traditions to separate the two. There is the root of faith in some experience of the divine, some encounter with God, some awareness of transcendence, some moment of truth – there are many ways of expressing it, but the basic idea is that there is an awareness of that reality which many traditions call God (and some don't). And then there is the development: the attempt to express and make sense of the experience. This is a matter of intellectual endeavor, worked out by human beings, using their reason and using the tools provided by their education and culture.

This is a distinction rooted in study of religious traditions – we have very briefly used Christianity as an example – and has been well drawn out by the theologian Wilfred Cantwell Smith, who makes the distinction between "faith" and "belief" or "religion". So far we have tended to use these words pretty much interchangeably, as most people do, but we shall have to be a bit more careful for a while. Cantwell Smith speaks of "faith" as a combination of experience and attitude: an awareness of being in relationship with the transcendent and being confronted by transcendent Reality. He believes that all humans have the capacity for faith, and that faith is a universal feature of human life, shared by all. Whether people talk in terms of the God of Abraham, Isaac, and Jacob or the supreme power of Brahman or just of "the way things are", they are talking about their experience of faith. Whether they meditate before the Western Wall or tie a prayer stick to a tree or perform the Hajj or visit the shrine of Our Lady at Walsingham, they are engaging in activities which express this universal faith; and so were the Romans when they made the obligatory sacrifices to Jupiter on the Capitol, and the Alexandrians who flocked to the Temple of Isis. And so on, and so on.

So why is all this religious talk so diverse, if the experience which it expresses is universal? Why are all these practices so diverse if they all arise out of this universal faith? The answer lies in the quite distinct phenomenon which Cantwell Smith calls belief or religion. Faith needs to be expressed and explained in particular places at particular times. Awareness of the transcendent is a universal experience, but it needs to be made sense of in the language and the culture of a particular people. Faith needs to be expressed in concepts and belief systems: and just as there is infinite variety in aspects of human culture down the ages and across the world, so there is a huge variety in the ways humans express their faith. And in the light of new experience of the transcendent, the ways faith is expressed and understood keep developing.

I think this is a very helpful way of understanding the distinction between the awareness of God which lies at the heart of faith, and the work of humans in trying to articulate their understanding of that awareness. Even if you are not persuaded by Cantwell Smith's assertion that every belief system is a response to the same basic human awareness of God, this does not mean that the distinction does not stand up between the encounter with God, and the words and concepts by which humans try to make sense of it. I think that distinction is right, and very helpful. On the basis of it, we can work out a reasonable attitude to the belief systems of religions.

But first, let us consider what might have been the consequences if a figure with similar impact to Jesus had emerged in a native American context; or among Australian aboriginals; or among the tribespeople of the Masai. He could still have been recognized as a figure uniquely related to the divine, and confronting humans with the challenge of relating to the divine; but the words and concepts in which this was expressed and remembered and recorded would have been very different from the words and concepts of the religious traditions of Israel and the philosophies of the Hellenistic world. They would have been conditioned by a quite different culture and expressed in a quite different way. And once we realize this, it is not so hard to see how very different systems of belief and theology could in fact originate in awareness of the same reality.

So let's go back to our brief look at Christianity. We left the early Christians arguing over theology: trying to work out exactly how to make sense of their faith-experience of Jesus. They came up in due course with some really clever theology: finely tuned systems of belief, creeds, and doctrinal statements, which were all developments of the attempts by the first followers of Jesus to make sense of their experience. Decades after the death of Jesus, they began writing down their memories and interpretations of his life. Decades after that, they gradually worked out which were the writings about Jesus that they wanted to keep as authoritative records, and which were the bits of good theology that they wanted to keep as authoritative guidance for further development; and in so doing they created the official collection of writings which we now know as the New Testament. There was a lot of stuff which did not get in, of course, from bizarre stories about Jesus' childhood to sophisticated theology influenced by Gnostic Greek cults which departed too far from Hebrew ideas about the goodness of God.

What did get in, though, was hardly a unity in itself. You can find many ways of understanding Jesus in the New Testament, and scholars have spent much time teasing out the different strands of the early Christians' thinking. A famous New Testament scholar, Ernst Kasemann, summed things up well when he said: "The New Testament canon does not, as such, constitute the foundations of the unity of the Church; on the contrary, it provides the basis for the multiplicity of the confessions." (Kasemann, E, Essays on New Testament Themes, London, 1964, p 103.) The New Testament gave Christians a number of ways to go in trying to understand Jesus, but it also set the boundaries. Gnostic theology, which made Jesus the representative of a good spiritual God trying to save humans from the power of the lesser God who created this earth, was too far out of line. Silly stories like those in the Infancy Gospel of Thomas about Jesus making sparrows out of mud and then bringing them to life were too trivial to take seriously. The boundaries were set, according to the wisdom and good sense of the leaders of the churches who gradually decided on the books that would be included or excluded.

Not that the formation of the New Testament put an end to the problems. No Christian can be unaware of the strife that has gone on throughout the Church's history, as one group claims the moral and theological high ground and condemns another. Doctrinal refinements have been worked out in discussion and argument and controversy over many years, sometimes with prayerful devotion and sometimes with bitter strife and accusations of heresy. One group which believes that the Son of God was not co-eternal with God, but was his first creation, loses an argument at a Council of the Early Church and is declared heretical and excommunicated. Seventeen centuries later, the Episcopal Church of the USA is condemned by other groups within the Anglican Communion for its refusal to discriminate on the grounds of gender or sexual orientation. In each case, both sides draw the grounds of their positions from Scripture, and each side claims that the other is fundamentally misrepresenting Scripture. It would seem that Scripture did not set the boundaries tightly enough to avoid controversy.

The process of development was not made any easier by the fact that Christians kept on having faith-experiences! And in trying to make sense of the new awareness given in these, they have kept further modifying and developing and re-defining the tradition. The Protestant Reformation was rooted in such developments, based on the faith-experience of certain key leaders, and the prophetic message which they believed it brought to the Church of their time. Several centuries down the line, Protestant theologies are very different in certain respects from the Catholic system of belief. Although we have grown beyond open conflict, except where it is more about politics than religion, there is still considerable suspicion between many Protestants and Roman Catholics at grass-roots level, reflecting the history of condemnation and counter-condemnation between the two groups over centuries of conflict.

When I was ordained in Birmingham Cathedral in 1984, I had to sign what is called a "declaration of assent". I had to repeat it in front of my new congregation before I could begin work in my first parish. I have it in front of me now. I declared my belief in "the faith which is revealed in the holy scriptures and set forth in the Catholic creeds, and to which the historic formularies of the Church of England bear witness". Elsewhere in the document, those "historic formularies" are defined as including the Thirty-nine Articles of Religion and the Book of Common Prayer. It is instructive to have a look at these and see exactly what I signed up to!

The Articles of Religion, agreed in 1562, used to be central to the Church of England's understanding of itself. I even own a clerical cassock which has thirty-nine buttons down the front, one for each of the Articles! I always say that button number 19 is my favorite, especially when talking to my Roman Catholic friends. This is because of Article 19, "Of the Church", which begins with a reasonable if slightly idealistic statement (as long as you remember that inclusive language was not a big issue in 1562!):

> "The visible Church of Christ is a congregation of faithful men, in the which the pure Word of God is preached, and the Sacraments be duly ministered according to Christ's ordinance...."

And it then goes on with my favorite bit:

> "As the Church of Jerusalem, Alexandria, and Antioch have erred; so also the Church of Rome hath erred, not only in their living and manner of Ceremonies, but also in matters of Faith."

Why do I draw attention to this? Because it is notable that among just thirty-nine statements intended to define true religion and true doctrine, one is devoted to saying who else is wrong! Not what is right, but who is wrong. And this reminds me of what I call the occupational hazard of religion – the readiness to say other people are wrong. And this in due turn reminds me of the imperfection of the human beings who drew up these formularies and worked on these doctrinal statements. All of us who care about theology and truth and right relations between people of faith are also imperfect human beings. We are flawed precisely because we are human. We are constrained by the limits of our intelligence and by the limits of our faith and by the limits of our empathy and sympathy. We are constrained by our own preoccupations, squabbles, priorities, and self-importance. Is it any wonder that the theology we produce is itself far from perfect, and requires constant re-working? Is it any wonder indeed that the theology any humans produce is flawed, incomplete, slanted, distorted? Would it not be far more surprising if it were not?

And here we build something more into our distinction, borrowed from Cantwell Smith, between faith and religion. Faith, you remember, is seen as an encounter with God, and therefore an awareness of Truth. But religion, with its belief-systems and its creeds and its condemnations of others, is a work of fallible human beings working within all the constraints of both their culture and their nature. And as a work of fallible human beings, we must accept that at best it will be far from complete and at worst it may be deeply flawed.

This is not really very surprising, when you consider what the subject-matter is. Cantwell Smith found it hard, as I have, to find the right words to explain the 'faith' side of his distinction. This is precisely because, when we begin to deal with God, or Reality, or the Transcendent, we hit the problem that it is very hard to describe something, or someone, so complex. At the start of the twentieth century, Rudolf Otto was studying religious experience, after a formative experience of his own. He came up with certain terms and phrases that are still central to study of this area, and which illustrate the difficulty of pinning it down with language. He described the sense of wonder with which, on hearing prayers in a synagogue in Tunis, he felt himself in the presence of what he called the "mysterium tremendum et fascinans" – roughly speaking, a terrifying and fascinating mystery. In his ground-breaking book "The Idea of the Holy", he talked a lot about this non-rational or supra-rational core of religion. He used another Latin idea, that of the "numen" or divinity, to coin the term "numinous", which he used to describe this mystery. With "numinous" are associated the ideas of awe and wonder, otherness, and not a little obscurity! Otto realized this: he suggested that the numinous could not be directly described, but could only be suggested or pointed to. No wonder that attempts to pin down the numinous in the categories of human theology have been so hard!

Another term which surfaces in the study of religious experience is "ineffable": meaning "beyond the grasp of our conceptual systems". It is applied both to authentic religious experience, and to God. Within Christian tradition there has always been a strand of thinking that has emphasized the ineffable nature of God. At a time when controversies over precisely how to talk about the nature of God and of the Christ were well advanced, the Cappadocian theologian Gregory of Nyssa wrote that God is: "incapable of being grasped by any term, or any idea, or any other device of our apprehension, remaining beyond the reach not only of the human but of the angelic and all supramundane intelligence, unthinkable, unutterable, above all expression in words". (Gregory of Nyssa, Against Eunomius, 1.42.)

It is a shame that those who were deeply engaged in controversy did not pay more attention to this idea. For usually the best arguments in the controversies were the ones that showed how inadequate or misleading the opposition's words about God were. Not surprisingly; for it is far easier to show how inadequate someone else's view is, than to construct a view oneself that is not inadequate! If all parties had been prepared to recognize that their own views were inadequate and partial too, progress in theological definitions might have been less painful.

Later on Thomas Aquinas, the father of Catholic theology, taught that when we use a word (e.g. "good") to describe God, we have to be using it in a quite different sense from how we use it when we talk about humans, because God is quite different in nature from anything else we might call "good". Islam has a similar principle about the ninety-nine names of God; they all describe him, but in a quite different sense from how they would describe a human. God the Judge is very different from any human judge, for instance, because human judges are fallible and God is believed to be infallible. But then you have to ask whether the word "infallible" is itself being used in a different sense; and suddenly you realize how difficult it is to say anything about God. Aquinas believed you could build up a partial understanding if you realized that adjectives like "good" are applied to God by analogy. That is, we can realize something about the goodness of God if we think of him as 'like' the most good person we know; but we are only getting a very impoverished, incomplete picture of the goodness of God from this.

Which reminds us again that any picture of God or theory about God expressed in human language is going to be impoverished and incomplete. Theologians are often prepared to acknowledge this: Professor Keith Ward for instance states in his essay "Divine Ineffability" (in Sharma A (ed), God, Truth and Reality, London 1993, p 219) that "there is a spiritual reality of supreme power and value; but we are unlikely to have a very adequate conception of it". And if our perception and our understanding are incomplete, then we need to keep on working at them. There is no sense in which theology is established or "finished". There is a very illuminating pair of books by the Oxford theologian Maurice Wiles whose titles together make the point. Wiles wrote an excellent book on the enterprise of the Church Fathers in the Patristic period – the first four centuries – entitled "The Making of Christian Doctrine". I remember using it extensively when writing essays for my tutor at university. It gave a clear view of the process by which the Fathers gradually worked towards the ideas summarized in the Creeds, and in the findings of the official Councils of the Church. Wiles made it exciting to trace the process by which they developed the niceties of Christian doctrine, using the philosophical ideas and categories of their time. Then, rather later, he followed it with "The Remaking of Christian Doctrine", arguing that Christians in the 20th century should be engaged in the same process, using the ideas and categories of our very different time to make sense of Christian doctrine for a very different world.

This has always been quietly going on, of course, even without Wiles arguing for it. Archbishop Rowan Williams, speaking at Birmingham University in 2003 on "Christian Theology and Other Faiths", argued passionately for the importance of keeping our eyes fixed on doctrine as well as practice when we consider our approach to other faiths. But he admitted straight away: "Our doctrine is still in formation", and by so doing opened up the possibility that it may be further formed in relationship with, not just in opposition to, other religious traditions.

If you doubt that our doctrine is still in formation, consider the ways in which our thinking as Christians in the twenty-first century differs from that of a few centuries ago. In the mid-nineteenth century, there was a huge controversy over the implications for Christian belief of Darwin's theories about evolution and the origin of species. Not only did his theory of the evolutionary relationship between humans and apes cast doubt on the special status of humanity as "made in God's image", but his theory of the development of life on earth required rather more than the six thousand years or so of the Biblical time-scale from creation to present day. Many Christians ceased to believe because the authority of the Bible for them was fatally weakened. Yet now in this country, most Christians are happy to accept the scientific hypotheses of the Big Bang and the process of evolution, and to hold the faith that God initiated and sustains the process. They are happy to follow the guidance of Biblical scholars, and to regard the first few chapters of Genesis as stories which are not literally true, but which contain important insights into the relationship between God and humanity, and into the nature of humanity. Christianity has not vanished from the earth because of Darwin, but theology did go through a paradigm shift.

Again, the doctrine of Hell. Family tradition indicates that my missionary great-grandfather was able to preach a pretty hot hell-fire sermon, giving a graphic description of the unpleasant consequences of failure to convert to Christianity. He could pick up on various New Testament hints about fire, and torment, and weeping and gnashing of teeth; and there were plenty of almost pornographic mediaeval descriptions of Hell of which a well-read man could scarcely be unaware. I am not wishing to imply that he dwelt unduly on this (though I do wish I had an example of the sermons!), and records indicate that his missionary activity was largely in the field of education and health care, so he was advocating Christianity in a positive way. But it is fair to say that this was the prevalent idea of hell at the time: and it is not now. Christians may talk of non-being or of separation from God, but most of us do not talk about torment in fire. No longer do we think in terms of the categories of Jewish apocalyptic literature, nor is our idea of Hell colored by the continually smoldering fires of the Jerusalem corporation dump in the valley of Hinnom.

Thirdly, and more controversially, attitudes towards women in ministry, and towards homosexuality in Christians and in Christian leaders, are changing. It was an unthinkable thing two generations ago that a woman, or a man in an openly gay relationship, might exercise the ministry of a Bishop in the Anglican Communion. Of course, there are many who vehemently oppose this development. For that matter, there are many who hold to every Biblical detail of the lake of fire prepared for the devil and his angels, and who believe that the earth was created in 4004 BC complete with every species of beast, and Adam and Eve in the Garden. But these groups within the Churches are fighting a rearguard action, as some groups always have. Doctrine develops, teaching changes, as Christian leaders and Christian people try to stay faithful to the heart of their faith in a changing world.

John Hick makes a similar point by drawing on research into mediaeval Christianity, and comes to a conclusion that at first sight seems astonishing:

> "When we compare their religious outlook a thousand years ago with ours in the mainline churches today, we find that, apart from the institutional continuity of the Church, there is hardly anything in common beyond our use of the same great symbols. For us today God is, above all, infinite love. For them God was a remote, arbitrary, terrifying power. The contrast could hardly be greater. Whereas we see ourselves as the children of a heavenly Father, they saw themselves as serfs of an all-powerful Lord whose honor was offended by their disobedience, so that most men and women were destined to the torments of hell." **(The Rainbow of Faiths, 1995, p 127)**

Yet really this is not so surprising: different times, different lives, different societal structures, different role models, produce a different idea of God. Hick goes on to show how, following scholarly research into the historical Jesus, the general Christian picture of Jesus has changed from emphasis on his power and glory as Son of God to emphasis on his humanity, vulnerability, and solidarity with the poor. This is the Jesus who inspires the Church's "bias to the poor", and appeals to the liberation theologians and the social

reformers. This is not the Jesus of the mediaeval church who sat en-
throned on high, surrounded by the heavenly host and the symbols
of divine power. Times change, experience changes, doctrines and
understandings change.

And even if we take a "snapshot" at a particular point and then
hold on to that point, as Christianity did with the New Testament
canon or the Nicene Creed, the way that we understand it changes.
Biblical scholarship does not stay static; and no Christian who re-
peats the Nicene creed and affirms belief in one Lord Jesus Christ
will have the same understanding of – say "begotten, not made"
or "being of one substance with the Father" as the fourth-century
Bishops had when they approved these subtle formulae for subtle
reasons of their own.

Understandings change. Theologies change. Religions go
through static periods and periods of change and development, in
response to the context they find themselves in. This was recognized even in that "Declaration of Assent" to which I alluded earlier.
For alongside the requirement to affirm loyalty to the "inheritance
of faith" was the recognition that this is a faith which we are "called
upon to proclaim afresh in each generation". Implicit here is the
principle that development is necessary, but it must remain faithful
to the spirit of what has gone before. This is something of a balancing act, weighing necessary innovation on the one hand against
loyalty to the past on the other. It is a balancing act which different
Christians will do very differently. What seems to Christian A to be
loyalty to the tradition may seem to Christian B like being stuck in
the past. On the other hand, B's necessary innovation may seem to
A like giving in to the trends of the modern world; and of course C's
paradigm shift may seem to D like abandoning the central pillars of
the religion!

And yet this too is part of the development of the religious world.
Central pillars do cease to be seen as central. Religions even fade
away completely. One of the most formative experiences of my
teenage years was traveling to the Eastern Mediterranean during
the years when I was studying the classical world, and seeing the
ruins of Mycenae and the walls of Troy, and the glorious ruins of

more Greek temples than I could count, from Athens to Ephesus and from Olympia to Delphi. I used to imagine these places full of worshippers, buzzing with expectation and awe as the priests and devotees performed the rituals and obligations which gave structure to their lives. And miles from all this, I visited the Temple of Mithras at Carrawburgh on Hadrian's Wall, and thought of the devotees of a Persian cult which gained popularity in the Roman military, comforting themselves in the alien environment of Northumbria with the familiar rituals of their religion.

Yet for all their influence, these religions are dead and gone, like many others. Some lasted thousands of years, like the religion of Pharaonic Egypt; some rather less. They must have seemed as solid as rock to their adherents and devotees; and yet now they are gone, and their only legacy is glorious ruins and references in ancient texts. Who is to say that any religious tradition is permanent? We have seen how the tradition of Christianity has evolved and changed; who knows what the future holds? We can be sure that the truth will not change; but the way we express it may well do so beyond recognition. To use Cantwell Smith's distinction, faith may be a universal feature of human life, but religion can change and develop with its changing context.

The upshot of all this should be clear. A religion, as a human response to God, is a system constructed by human beings. Religions are human constructs. Their scriptures are human constructs, written by humans and kept, treasured, and interpreted by humans. Their theologies, doctrines, creeds, are human constructs, expressed in the human language of a particular time and place, and using the human categories and concepts of that particular time and place. Over time they develop in response to change; sometimes slowly and smoothly, sometimes fast and abruptly. Sometimes they are revolutionized by paradigm changes. Sometimes they are challenged to their foundations by the changing world of which they are part. But if they respond to the challenge by developing, they can continue to give human beings a way of understanding and approaching God, and making God meaningful in their lives. They can continue to function as the link between God and their particular context, even as that context itself changes.

Admitting that religions are constructed by human beings does not mean that they lack value or meaning. Each religious tradition can serve as a link between humanity and that Reality which we in the Christian tradition approach as God. Each is rooted in a faith-response to that Reality; each develops through continuing faith-responses to that Reality in a context which is shaped by the tradition and in turn keeps on re-shaping that tradition. In this respect, each tradition has immense value and meaning for those whose lives are shaped by it, and it is quite natural for its followers to feel immense loyalty and zeal for it.

But admitting that religions are constructed by human beings *does* mean that they lack absolute status. If we accept this analysis of religions, we can no longer say "We are right, you are wrong" – but *nor can anyone else*. No religious tradition can claim absolute status. No religious tradition can claim to be the one by which all others are to be judged.

But all religious traditions may find the grounds for a positive view of others within this analysis. For if all religions are attempts to make sense of religious experiences or faith-responses, or indeed simply of the nature of the physical and spiritual world around us, then all may have valuable insights. All may have things to teach the others, and things to learn from the others. We may treasure our own tradition, and it is right and natural that we should. But at the same time we should remember that it is our tradition only because of the accident of our birth, the family and social context into which we were born. And it is only the tradition it is because of the accident of *its* birth in a particular place, time, and context.

So where does this leave us? We have ended up with a view of religious traditions as constructed by human beings. We have worked out that if this is right, no religion has a right to claim absolute status. In other words, no religion has a right to start any statement about itself and others with the phrase: "We are right, and you ....". Which rules out the positions which we examined in chapters two, three, and four. Yet we felt that the position of chapter five was not quite satisfactory either. It had the merit of leveling off the religious traditions, so that no longer was one claiming priority; but it seemed to allow equality of truth-claims rather too easily. Is there another approach we can try?

8

None of us is valueless

By the end of the last chapter, we had reached the point of suggesting that there is value in all religious systems, because they all represent human responses trying to express an understanding of the reality which they encounter in faith. We had also noted that all religious systems tend to undergo development and change, as they adapt to changing contexts and to the changing needs of their believers. This book is suggesting that now is the time for one important change: a radical change in our attitude to those who believe differently from ourselves. Note the word radical. It is carefully chosen. It is generally used these days in the sense of "drastic" or "revolutionary", and certainly for some Christians the changes I suggest will be drastic indeed. But the word is derived from the Latin "radix", "root", and so a "radical" change could be taken as one that is deeply rooted in the tradition, or one which involves returning to the roots of the tradition. It is fair to say that although religious traditions can be open to revolutionary changes, they tend to be far happier with developments that can be shown to be in continuity with their existing tradition. A change that is "radical" in both senses has far more chance than one which is radical in the first sense alone.

So, since we seem to be moving towards accepting the value of all religious traditions, the question must be faced: is this development in line with anything in existing Christian tradition? Is a change to valuing other religious traditions a radical change in both senses? To answer this, we must have a look back through elements of Christian thinking and teaching, and also look at certain key elements of Scripture.

To take the thinking and teaching first, this acceptance of traditions beyond our own is far from new. In chapter four we looked at the "Logos" theology of Justin the Martyr in the second century. He was one of the group of theologians who earned the title "Apologists" – a word which has nothing to do with being sorry! The Apologists were concerned to present a balanced, reasoned, and attractive view of Christianity to the Greek world of their time, and to argue against the slander that Christianity was only fit for the credulous and the stupid. Justin deals at one point in his Apology with the question of "Who are true Christians?" Using his "Logos" theology, he identifies the Christ with the Word (Logos) of God, and the Word of God with human reason (logos), "in which the whole human race shares". Then he makes his bold statement: "And those who have lived in accordance with Reason are Christians" (Justin, First Apology, 46.2). This is a massive assertion: that every soul which has borne witness through reason to the Good and the Ideal is in fact a Christian. Perhaps they are not perfect Christians: but then again, who is? The important factor is that these people can claim the name of Christian by virtue of a kind of contact with God which is available to the whole human race, whether or not they have ever heard the name of Jesus.

Justin does investigate the question of why those who live in accordance with reason disagree on many issues and even contradict each other. He comes up with the idea that the philosophers of Greece have only a partial knowledge of the truth, because their knowledge of the Logos is only partial. Their views are distorted: whereas Christians have received the full revelation and therefore have the whole truth. In this Justin unashamedly sets Christianity at the pinnacle and uses it as a standard by which to judge the philosophers, and of course he finds them lacking in certain respects – though some, like Socrates and Heraclitus, come very close. He is a generous inclusivist, rather than a pluralist, but he opens up the way to pluralism. Once it is admitted that even Christianity has only a partial understanding of the truth, and is still trying to develop its understanding of God, then Justin's inclusivism becomes a celebration of plurality. Every contact with the revelation of God in his creation, through the exercise of reason, becomes to some extent at least a valid response to God. What is more, every such contact becomes something which helps to build up a fuller picture of God and God's relationship with humanity.

So there is precedent in Justin's Logos theology for an approach which celebrates true insight into God, wherever and whenever it is found, and whatever name it goes by. It should be noted of course that during the same century there were other developments in Christianity going on at the same time, but of a very different nature. Other Christian leaders were dealing with Greek influences in a very different way: not developing a positive response to the teaching of the great philosophers, but dealing with the threat of false and corrupting teaching from Gnostic sects. This led them to answer the question "Who are true Christians?" in a very different fashion. They set up a system of testing for orthodoxy by two criteria: submission to legitimate authority and assent to orthodox statements of doctrine. It became important of course at this point to define legitimate authority and to define true doctrine; and so the Church became characterized by strict definitions and clear boundaries. A religious institution was emerging, which had little in common with the generous and open celebration in Justin's theology of the Logos "in which the whole human race shares".

These two conflicting attitudes – one encouraging institutional conformity and one celebrating plurality – have been in tension ever since. Often the celebration of plurality has been a minority view, but it has never died out, and at times it has found outspoken champions. Hick, among others, has delighted in appealing to them, and I am indebted to his discussion in "The Rainbow of Faiths", starting on page 34. One of the most notable is the fifteenth-century cardinal Nicholas of Cusa, who wrote in his treatise on "Peace between Faiths" that "each system possesses a certain degree of truth", and "only through a study of the various systems can one have an inkling of the unity of the unattainable truth". Remarkable for a cardinal of the Roman Catholic Church, you may think; but like many another he bases his religious understanding on an experience which forces him to confront a challenge. He tells of a vision in which he saw "a vast system of religious unity" emerging from diversity, and saw contributions made by "a Greek, an Italian, a Hindu, an Arab, a Chaldaean, a Jew, a Scythian, a Persian, a Syrian, a Spaniard, a Tartar, a German, a Bohemian, and last of all an Englishman". Last but not least, we English must hope! Here is an outstanding celebration of plurality which sees representatives of different religious systems and widely divergent cultures all contributing to building up the bigger picture.

The New World too, with its proud principles of religious freedom, contributed to this honorable strand of Christian tradition. The founder of Pennsylvania, the Quaker William Penn, expressed similarly positive views of the devout followers of diverse traditions in his "Some Fruits of Solitude" (1786):

> "The humble, meek, merciful, just, pious and devout
> souls are everywhere of one religion: and when death has
> taken off the mask they will know one another, though the
> divers liveries they wear here makes them strangers."

Here is something not very far from the distinction between faith and religion which we met in Cantwell Smith: the faith is universal and is expected to bring people together, but the ways the faith is dressed up in systems and doctrines vary so much that the people of faith become strangers to one another.

Of course, those to whom such teaching appeals will always find themselves up against the boundary-drawers. Those who see the limits of salvation as determined by the limits of the Christian Church will be less than happy with Justin and his Logos-theology, and downright unhappy with the celebration of plurality in Nicholas of Cusa or William Penn.

Which leaves me asking myself: what is more Christian, to draw clear boundaries and exclude those who fall beyond them, or to celebrate the awareness of God wherever it is found? What is more Christian, to demand that a person sign up to a series of orthodox doctrinal statements to be considered "sound", or to celebrate their love of God and their neighbor, however they express their beliefs? What is more Christian, to say that only those who define the Spirit of God as the third person of God proceeding from the Father and the Son are right, or to respond with open arms to those who are moved by the Spirit of God, however they understand and refer to him/her/it?

Let us have a look at a few New Testament clues, from the recorded attitudes of Jesus to boundaries and definitions. I teach the Gospel of Mark to mixed-faith groups, and have to spend quite a lot of time setting it in its context. We consider both the time of Jesus' life and ministry, and the time and context in which it is thought to have been written, sometime in the sixties during the Roman persecution in the time of the Emperor Nero. We consider what the author was trying to achieve, and the ways in which he edits and selects his material; we consider his bias against certain Jewish groups, and the way in which he tries to clear Pilate the Roman governor of the blame for the death of Jesus. And of course, we consider the possibility of a certain pro-Jesus bias.

And yet after all this is taken into consideration, my able students of various faiths and none, many of whom have never encountered Gospel material before, are left with a powerful impression not only of Jesus, but of the attitudes which he demonstrates and commends. Of course this impression is largely the result of careful presentation and editing on the part of Mark, but we can be in no doubt that it reflects the experience of one group of Jesus' followers, and presents the picture upon which at least this group of early Christians is agreed. And what is this picture?

From the very start of the gospel it is the picture of a man who is presenting people with an opportunity to change: to stop being content and to challenge themselves to think in new ways. The first recorded words of Jesus in the Gospel are a resounding challenge, echoing the challenge of John the Baptist: "The time has come, and the Kingdom of God is near! Turn away from your sins, and believe the Good News!" (Mark 1.15) Placed in this position by Mark for maximum impact, to sum up the message of Jesus, these words tell us that he expected God to act to bring in the Kingdom, but that he also challenged people to change so that they could become part of it. The people had to decide: were they going to be alive to the possibility that God might be in action around them, or were they going to stick to the same old ways?

Jesus' encounters, as narrated by Mark, fill out the ways in which he expected those around him to be alive to new opportunities. He challenges the fishermen, Simon and Andrew, James and John, to grasp the opportunity of a new and challenging way of life. As they and the rest of his followers move forward in understanding with him, he challenges them to extend their sympathies and their vision beyond the limits of what they have been taught. He challenges them to be at ease with the company of those whom they have previously considered to be outcast: that wonderful pairing of "tax collectors and sinners"! He challenges their attitude to women during their menstruation: when he is sought out and touched by a woman whose menstrual irregularity has made her "unclean" for the last twelve years, Jesus does not rebuke her for touching him and so making him unclean too, but instead commends her faith and sorts out her problem.

When his followers become preoccupied with questions about their own status or honor, he invariably takes them down a peg or two. James and John want to sit at his right hand and his left as his two chief sidekicks in the Kingdom, but they are told that they need to think differently; greatness is about service, not status. They need to think differently about Gentiles too: when the Syro-Phoenician woman challenges Jesus' reference to the Jewish-Gentile boundary, he crosses the boundary and makes himself available to her. His disciples do not welcome children to their company either, thinking that they will be a nuisance; but Jesus takes the opportunity to make a teaching point out of the incident, commenting that "the Kingdom of God belongs to such as these". There are many ways of interpreting this comment, but one is certainly to stress the open-mindedness and receptiveness of children. Unlike many adults, children are not set in their ideas, and they do not tend to think that they have it all worked out already. In all these incidents there is a common theme: that the followers of Jesus should be alive to new opportunity and new vision, should broaden out their vision and their understanding, and should be prepared to cross the man-made boundaries of their religious tradition.

Consistent with this picture is Jesus' position in theological dispute. Where there is dispute over the teaching of the Law or doctrinal matters such as the afterlife, Jesus tends to favor the viewpoint of the forward-looking Pharisees over the traditionalist teaching of the Sadducees: he draws on Messianic interpretations of prophecy, he teaches that there is an afterlife, and he expresses impatience with attention to the details of Temple ritual. At the same time, when there is a danger of the Law being applied with such attention to detail that the spirit of the Law is frustrated, he challenges the Pharisees and teachers of the Law to enlarge their vision still further. In Mark's account of the healing of a paralyzed man on the Sabbath, it is the stubbornness of the Pharisees that makes Jesus angry; his argument is better than theirs, but they will not admit it. We should note here in fairness that Mark presents an undeservedly negative image of the Pharisaic movement, but this cannot hide the common ground they share with Jesus any more than it can hide the challenge he presents to them. The Pharisees used to claim that they had "put a fence around the Law" for its protection: that is, they had surrounded it with such detailed guidance that it would be very hard for any devout Jew inadvertently to break it. Jesus challenges them (to adapt a piece of contemporary management jargon) to "think outside the fence". They need to remember the real purpose of the Sabbath, not just the regulations surrounding it. They need to remember that it is not the righteous people of Israel but the sinful and the outcast who most need to hear about God's care and to experience care from God's servants.

The message is clear. It is good to be open-minded and receptive to new ideas, and to be alive to the possibility that God may be working in unexpected ways and among unexpected people. To rest on old definitions without thinking about them or questioning them is dangerous. Just as Jesus challenges those who cling to the details of the Law while forgetting its overall thrust, so he challenges those who cling to ancient ritual or custom without taking account of the needs of the people around them. He turns over the tables of the Temple traders who are making money out of the ritual requirements of Temple worship, and he responds approvingly to the teacher of the Law who states that "To love God with all your heart, and with all your mind, and with all your strength, and to love your neighbor as yourself, is more important than to offer animals and other sacrifices to God". Like the children, this teacher of the Law is "not far from the Kingdom of God".

The Jesus of the earliest Gospel, then, is presented as one who breaks down boundaries and encourages an openness to the unexpected activity of God. That gives quite a strong nudge towards answering the question with which we started our quick look at Mark. It seems that seeking to transcend boundaries is more of a Jesus-centered approach than drawing them strictly and sheltering behind them.

That is all very well, you may be thinking now. That is quite a persuasive picture of some aspects of Jesus as portrayed in Mark. But what about those awkward texts which we looked at back in chapter two? What about Jesus being the way, the truth, and the life, and no-one coming to the Father except by him? What about there being no other name in heaven and earth by which we must be saved? And you are right if you are thinking that. Of course we must have another look at those. But first of all, let us remember what we said in chapter six about Scripture. We recognized the distinction between an encounter with transcendent reality, and the religious system which tries to make sense of that encounter in the categories of a particular time, place, and culture. The production of Scriptures is part of that process. Scriptures, we said, "are human constructs, written by humans and kept, treasured, and interpreted by humans". If this is the case, then it may also be the case that what was expressed to meet the needs of Christian communities struggling for survival and self-definition in the Hellenistic world may not be appropriate to the needs of very different Christian communities in a very different world. Nevertheless, it is still worth trying to understand the texts in context, to see if this is indeed the case.

Starting then with John chapter 14 verse 6: "I am the way, the truth, and the life: no one comes to the Father except by me." On the face of it this is pretty plain: these are the words of Jesus, and if we believe Jesus we have to believe this. Some people interpret this to mean that only those who confess Jesus as their personal Lord and Savior have any hope of salvation. This is back to "We are right, you are wrong". Some people go much more inclusive and say that anyone who comes to the Father is in fact coming via Jesus, even if they do not know it. This is back to "We are right, you are partly right (even if you don't know it)". But remember – the text needs to be set in its context. Who is actually speaking? This is the Gospel of John. This is not just the Gospel of the wandering Messianic preacher. This is the Gospel of the Logos incarnate, of the cosmic Christ who is also the light that enlightens every human. These are the words of that Logos which is available to every human being, at all times, in all places, in all cultures. Of course nobody comes to the Father except by the universal Logos which is available to all human beings. Seen in the context of John's theology, as expressed at the start of his Gospel so that every reader will grasp it, this is not limiting the availability of salvation at all. It is extending the boundary so that it gathers in everyone. Truly this is a celebration of God's availability to all.

The same message can be found in that other "proof-text" of exclusivism, Acts 4.12. "There is salvation in no one else, for there is no other name under heaven given among men by which we must be saved." The context of this remark is the defense of Peter, who has been hauled before the most powerful of the Sadducees to answer questions about his subversive activities. "By what power", he is asked, "or by what name did you do this (ie this healing)?" And his answer is "by the name of Jesus Christ of Nazareth, whom you crucified, whom God raised from the dead". No surprise here; we would expect nothing else. But Peter is clear that the source of the power is God. God has raised Jesus from the dead; God has healed a crippled man, through the name of that same Jesus. What is more, Peter is responding to a specific question about a specific incident, and about himself and his companions. His statement in verse twelve is usually taken as a general comment about salvation, but it is unnatural to take it this way. It is much more natural to take it in context as a statement about this particular incident, this particular healing. The Greek word "soteria" can mean "salvation" in the technical Christian sense, but it can also mean "saving", "preservation", "deliverance" or "release" in the sense of release from captivity or from illness – which of course is exactly what Peter has just been asked about. So he can say defiantly to the high priest that the man was delivered from illness by the name of Jesus, and that the name of Jesus is sufficient among this group for such things to happen. No other name is needed: "And this deliverance is not through anyone else: for there is no other name under heaven given among men, by which *we* need to be delivered." The name of Jesus is proclaimed to be sufficient for healing; no other is required. Even if Peter is talking about salvation in the theological sense after all, however unnatural it is to shift to this meaning, we should still note he talks about "we". This has usually been taken, when the text is detached from its context, as meaning we, the human race; but in context it is far more natural to take it as Peter referring to himself and his companions as "we". That name, he says, is sufficient for us, the followers of Jesus of Nazareth. This does not imply, however, that it is necessary for all. The possibility is still left open that for others there are other ways.

So even the proof-texts of exclusivism can bear other interpretations, when set in context. They do not necessarily restrict the boundaries of truth or of salvation to the orthodox Christian who is prepared to sign on the dotted line and agree to a string of sound doctrinal propositions. In John chapter 14 verse 6 we find a splendid proclamation of the universally accessible grace of God, and even in the words of Peter in Acts we find a robust personal statement of response to God which does not of itself rule out the validity of other responses.

So even if we take seriously the force of these texts, as long as we see them in their context, we do not find that an openness to plurality is ruled out. We should still remember that scriptures are written by humans, and may have all the shortcomings of anything created by humans. It is often said that scriptures are like witness-statements, and the force of the Gospels is partly down to their dependence on original eye-witness accounts of Jesus' ministry which lay at the heart of the oral tradition of early Christian teaching. Yet anyone who has ever dealt with witness-statements to a road traffic accident or a criminal act will know that there are as many different versions as there are witness-statements, and that no single detail of any one statement can carry very much weight on its own. We should remember this too when we are tempted to lay huge emphasis on one reported sentence uttered in the gospels by Jesus or in the book of Acts by Peter. Nevertheless the Scriptures are the repositories of the insights and understandings upon which Christianity is founded, and it is reassuring to know that even an openness to pluralistic possibilities is not ruled out by the tradition.

Indeed we may finish where the Bible finishes – in the book of Revelation, which is a product of the cryptic tradition of Jewish visionary writing about the end of the world and the triumph of God, adapted to a Christian context. In the final chapters of the book of Revelation, the writer describes his vision of the City which represents the final state of God's creation. There is no Temple worship in this City; religions have passed away, and there is only God, and the Lamb who in the vision represents the Christ-figure, the light that has enlightened the nations of the world, the same that John the Evangelist called the Logos. The vision is a glorious celebration of the uniting of all things under God:

> "And I saw no temple in the City, for its temple is the Lord
> God the Almighty and the Lamb. And the city has no need
> of sun or moon to shine upon it, for the glory of God is
> its light, and its lamp is the Lamb. By its light shall the
> nations walk; and the kings of the earth shall bring their
> glory into it, and its gates shall never be shut by day – and
> there shall be no night there; they shall bring into it the
> honor and glory of the nations."

It is hard indeed to read that and fail to celebrate the response of all nations to truth, to reality, to God, however they express it. We can celebrate plurality in religion, while still remaining faithful to a strong strand of our Christian heritage.

9

None of us is completely right, and all of us may be wrong

"Concerning the gods, I have no means of knowing whether they exist or not or of what sort they may be. Many things prevent knowledge including the obscurity of the subject and the brevity of human life."

This cautionary statement is one of a few surviving fragments of the work of the Athenian philosopher Protagoras, and formed the opening sentence of his treatise "On the Gods". What a shame we don't have more of it. As long ago as the fifth century BC, Protagoras was maintaining that all you could be sure about was humanity. For observing that "man is the measure of all things" and for rejecting the cults of the gods, Plato reports that Protagoras was exiled by the people of Athens, and his books were publicly burned in the market-place. Such was the fate, even then, of those who challenged the claim that it is possible to know the truth about the divine.

The claim is pervasive in religious circles. In many Christian circles, the answer to the question "How do you claim to know this?" is "The Bible says so". As we used to sing in Sunday school,

"Jesus loves me, this I know
For the Bible tells me so."

That is fine until, as we have seen, we begin to ask what the Bible actually is. And when we see it as the record of three thousand years of attempts on the part of a religious community to understand the nature and the requirements of God, it is no longer quite so easy to pick bits out and say "The Bible says so". What it does tell us is the way many humans of great devotion and godliness have understood God and the demands of God; and that deserves to be taken with great seriousness, of course. But then so do the insights into the nature and requirements of God from people of great devotion and godliness in other traditions, who have produced other Scriptures arising from other cultures and other contexts.

We should be clear that what we have now, in any religious tradition, are *beliefs*. We do not know. We have no basis to claim that we *know* the truth about the nature of God. The most we can say is that we have strong beliefs based upon our upbringing or our experience and the way we interpret it. We can say we have convictions or that we are convinced; but this is very different from saying that we know. As we saw a while ago, there has always been an awareness that we do not have the full picture, because human language and human thinking are inadequate to express the complexity and the ineffability of God. There has always been an awareness that we have more to learn; if this is so, the flipside of the coin is that we do not have complete knowledge.

And if we do not have complete knowledge, then we should be very wary of claiming either that we know we are right, or even more that others are wrong. In fact, all the claims we examined earlier in the book that began "We are right" turn out to have been overstating the case a bit. If we do not know, then how can we claim we are right? If we have not got the full picture, how can we possibly claim to have the right picture, and that other people do not? We can claim we have a picture that we believe in passionately, of course. We can claim to have a picture that shapes our lives and leads us in the way that we believe is right. We can claim to have a picture that leads us to love God and our neighbor and to strive for justice to the poor and peace among the nations. We can even claim to have a picture that leads us to take a positive view of our neighbors' religion and makes us want to work with them and learn from them. But we cannot claim to have the full picture and we cannot claim to have the whole truth.

And it is a good thing to realize this. For the history of religions shows that it is when people start claiming to have the full picture, to know that they are right, that trouble starts. We have mentioned the Crusades and the Holy Inquisition as less than glorious episodes in the history of Christianity. Both arose from a burning sense of conviction that one group had the truth, and had the right to impose it on others. This same burning conviction that one group has the truth leads over and over again to tragic consequences: convictions about God and the Land of Israel, convictions about the need to convert the world by force, convictions about the rightness of the Sunni or the Shi'ite path. If we are to believe the Gospels, rigid convictions about the needs of the people of Judaea led to the crucifixion of Jesus. Wherever there is rigid dogmatism and absolute exclusivism, there is strife and tragedy following not far behind. We have noted that many clear-thinking people reject religion on the grounds of the evils that have been done in its name. It has often been noted in defense of religion that these evils tend to be worst when they are mixed up with political or territorial ambitions, which are not really about the religion at all. That is true; but it has been less often noted that war and brutality tend to follow when people claim certainty. If they believe they have access to some God-given right or truth which must not be challenged and to which everyone else ought to yield, then there may be no limit to the evil they will do in the service of that "right" or that "truth". The distorted version of Islam which led to the 9/11 attack on New York, and the 7/7 bombings in London, combines rigid certainty with a burning zeal for the cause. Able and devout young men are willing to die and to kill for this cause, all because of a mistaken belief that they *know*.

Despite their frequency, we must admit that claims to know are unfounded and misguided. Claims to be right can at best be partial, and must always admit that there is more that could be known. There is a certain humility in this admission which is itself in tune with Christian tradition. Even St Paul, not always noted for humility, has the good sense to tell the people of Corinth that what humans call knowledge is incomplete and imperfect, and must be regarded as such.

> "For our knowledge is imperfect and our prophecy is imperfect; but when the perfect comes, the imperfect will pass away.... For now we see in a mirror, dimly, but then we shall see face to face. Now I know in part; then I shall understand fully."
> (1 Corinthians 13.9–12)

Mirrors in the ancient world of course were not the pieces of precision engineering they are now, but were dim and dark, distorting the image that was viewed. Better than nothing, but not clear. Paul says that similarly what we fondly believe to be knowledge about God is dim, dark and distorted; better than nothing, but not clear. Interestingly, the phrase which is usually translated "darkly" or "dimly" is the Greek "en ainigmati", which is related to the English "enigma" and generally means a "riddle" – the link is in the idea of obscurity, as a riddle is something which obscures its true meaning. I think this is quite a useful insight into theology – that trying to talk sensibly about God is like trying to work out a puzzle, or a series of puzzles where one leads on to another. It is one of the complaints of my students when beginning to learn about the philosophy of religion, that every answer throws up more new questions. That is of course the excitement of it: every answer that is worked out challenges more assumptions and raises more new issues to consider. As the song "Rosie" says, which I have printed at the start of the book, "the more I learn, it's the less I seem to know". That is the experience of the philosopher as it is the experience of many followers of religion, myself included. The more we learn, the more we are brought face to face with the vast amount we do not know, and the less we find we can take for granted.

Anyway, back to Paul. He gives the Christians of Corinth, and indeed Christians down the ages, a salutary reminder. Human knowledge is partial and incomplete. It may therefore be a good foundation for further learning and for dialogue with other learners; but it is not a good ground to judge the "knowledge" of others. It is not, in other words, a good yardstick or checklist by which others can be judged and found wanting. This fits in very well with certain wise remarks in the Gospels about the danger of judging others, which apply as well to intellectual claims as to moral ones. Jesus gives advice on judgment in Matthew 7.1–5:

> "Judge not, that you be not judged. For with the judgment
> you pronounce will you be judged, and the measure you
> give will be the measure you get. Why do you see the
> speck that is in your brother's eye, but not the log that
> is in your own eye? Or how can you say to your brother,
> 'Let me take the speck out of your eye', when there is the
> log in your own eye? You hypocrite, first take the log out
> of your own eye, and then you will see clearly to take the
> speck out of your brother's eye."

Which is to say: Get your own act together before you start worrying about setting other people straight. Too often it is easy to sit in judgment on others while remaining blissfully unaware of what is wrong with ourselves. The advice works on the level of any individual relationship, including the relationship between believers of different religious traditions.

I believe we should all be far more aware of the potential "log" in our own eye. When we admit that even our own cherished traditions and ways of understanding are part of a religious system made by humans in response to something we cannot fully understand, then we have moved away from the kind of superior judgment that began "We are right". We have renounced the right to make a judgment about others on the basis of being right ourselves. Instead we are saying something very different. We are admitting that our cherished traditions and ways of understanding are *provisional*. They are our best shot yet; but they are not the full picture. We are admitting that we still have much to learn; and maybe even some things to unlearn.

It may be helpful to explain that I am viewing religious systems here as something like scientific hypotheses. We have seen how John Hick and the pluralists borrowed the idea of the paradigm shift from the history of scientific method, and I think that is a very helpful suggestion. To build on it, I believe we should see each developed religious view as a hypothesis – a theory constructed in the light of experience to give the best possible fit to the available evidence. This is consistent with our examination of the nature of religious traditions in chapter six, and makes sense of the way in which they have developed. A good hypothesis is a close fit to the evidence, making sense of all the strands of the evidence and relating them together. It may become extremely widely accepted, but it is still no more than a hypothesis; and there is always the possibility that it may need to be modified, supplemented, or even replaced in the light of further evidence or a better explanation of the evidence. Even if it is very helpful to the development of science, and extremely illuminating, no good scientist will regard a hypothesis as any more than provisional. I believe this is exactly the way we should regard religious traditions: as attempts to make sense of the evidence, using the words and concepts available at the time, and modified in the light of further developments. I believe further that increased awareness of the merits of other traditions may be regarded as a new piece of evidence, which may require that we modify our understanding – just as new scientific evidence leads to scientific understanding being developed.

Of course, sometimes scientists forget that their theories are only hypotheses, or they stop treating them as such. Sometimes they start demanding that we believe them unconditionally. This happened recently in the context of the debate over teaching about creation in schools, when Dr Richard Pike, chief executive of the British Royal Society of Chemistry, said that children should be taught evolution not as a theory but as a fact. References to it being a theory should be abandoned, he said, as they gave the impression that there are valid alternative views.

> "Above all, we should no longer talk of the theory of evolution as though it is 'just an idea'. So well-established is it, that it now warrants the designation of an immutable scientific law, and should be taught as such. It is on this

basis that further dialogue should begin." **(Richard Pike, Friday April 21 2006)**

Here is science getting a little too big for its boots, and forgetting that scientific method is hypothetical. Here is science forgetting that certain equally well-established theories have been exploded by new evidence in the past. Here is science, ironically, doing exactly what scientists have criticized the churches for in the past – presenting received dogma as fact that must be believed. In effect, Pike is saying "Admit that I am right and then we can have dialogue – but the dialogue must be on my terms". I am led to note that "We are right, you are wrong" is just as unattractive in a scientific context as it was in a religious one.

If you are a responsible scientist, you should not try to get away with presenting a hypothesis, however well founded, as the last word on the subject. You should not try to present the provisional as certainty. And I believe the same applies in the case of religion. It is a mistake to present the provisional as though it is the last word. Better to remember St Paul on knowledge, and to learn the lessons both of history and of the world in which we live. In science as in religion, if the two parties to a dialogue both admit that they may have something to learn from the other, then there is ground for a fruitful discussion on an equal level. There is some point to dialogue then.

This point about hypotheses is well illustrated by a little parable which is a commonplace of writing about different faiths, but which I have managed to resist using until now. This is the story, originally found in Indian tradition but now found in many books on interfaith relations, of the six blind men who attempt to describe an elephant. One grasps the tail and says it is rather like a rope; another latches on to the leg and says it is rather like a tree-trunk, while a third tries to get hold of the trunk and suggests that he is wrestling with a snake. And so on! The blind men of course stand for different religious traditions, while the elephant represents God. People who do not like this parable say that liberals often use it to suggest that all religions are the same. Well, I am not using it like that; we have seen that religions are very different, and that some seem to lead to a better way of life than others. I want to say on the basis of this story that there is a strong possibility that all religions are responses to an encounter with the same reality; but if that is so, they have got hold of very different impressions of that reality. Why is that? It is because the elephant is much bigger than they are, and they cannot get the big picture. They only have a partial view. They are all of them right; but what they say is only partially true, and on its own it must be taken as provisional.

The story was rather engagingly put into verse by the Victorian poet John Godfrey Saxe, and I have reproduced it as the first appendix at the end of this book. It is worth quoting the key lines here, though, as they sum up the heart of the story:

> "And so these men of Indostan disputed loud and long,
> Each in his own opinion exceeding stiff and strong,
> Though each was partly in the right, and *all were in the wrong!*"

There is of course a problem with this story, useful though it is. In the story, the storyteller is looking at the whole incident, and can see the whole elephant. There is no-one however who can see the whole of God. So we have to accept that we are like the blind men: if we talk to each other, we can discover that we have each got hold of something bigger than ourselves. If we each accept that our understanding is provisional and incomplete, then we can learn from each other and put together a more complex picture. We may never quite get the shape of an elephant, but we shall become aware of more aspects of it, and we shall become more in awe of its complexity. On the other hand, if we start claiming that we are right about the elephant and everyone else is wrong, then we are in for a very hard time indeed, for we shall sink into the kind of sterile conflict that can never be resolved until we all stop insisting that we are right.

So as long as we remember that we are like the blind men and not like the storyteller, this little Indian story helps us see how each religious tradition may fit in to the bigger picture. Of course, as we have just said, there is no-one who is in a position to see the whole of the bigger picture, and therefore no-one who can say for certain that this is the way things are. But this fits perfectly with what we have been saying. Our religious views are hypotheses: and so is this. I believe firmly, however, that this view is a better fit to the evidence we have than any claim which says that one of these traditions is right and all the others are wrong. Unless a better hypothesis emerges, I will continue to believe and argue that we are all groping towards understanding of the same elephant, and that we have much to learn from each other in the process. If our understandings look very different, it is because we tend to try to reduce complexity to fit our own ideas, and because we approach the elephant from different angles, different contexts, different cultures.

I think I have probably pushed the elephant image far enough! But the point is clear. If we accept that our viewpoint is limited and our judgment is provisional, then we open up the possibility of learning from each other. Let us be clear what I am saying. I am of course commending a pluralist view; but it is not the kind of pluralism that appears to devalue truth and critical judgment by saying glibly "We are right and so are you". One of the reasons why that form of pluralism developed was because some Christians were rightly uncomfortable with any approach that said "We are right and you aren't". However generously these approaches viewed others, they always did so from a position of superiority, and so pluralism tried to put everyone on a level instead. As it were, it tried to raise everyone to the superior position. Everyone was right. Every competing truth-claim was good; every blind man was entirely correct in what he was saying. (Sorry, couldn't resist one more go at it!)

What I am commending is a slightly different view. I am suggesting that we put all religious traditions on an equal level, not by pulling them all up to the superior position, but by putting none of them in the superior position. Not even our own. We accept that all religious traditions including our own have come up with partial and provisional insights. They are expressed in hypotheses that may need to be changed and will certainly need continually to be developed in the light of experience – and that experience will include our experience of each other. It may require us to re-evaluate our own tradition, and work out afresh what is central and how it may best be expressed in our current context. It may require the incorporation of wisdom gleaned from other traditions. If we are willing to learn and develop together in the light of this kind of dialogue, then none of us can any longer be accused of seeking to be superior or to claim the high ground of exclusive access to truth. None of us is being arrogant, because we are starting from a position of humility and an acceptance that we have not got the whole truth.

This will involve a change in attitude for all of us, and it is not an easy one to grasp. It has crept up on me very gradually over a considerable number of years, and it is hard to express all its implications. Since part of it fell into place for me while listening to a folk concert at Symphony Hall in Birmingham, I propose to use the song in question to try to suggest some of the ways forward. If nothing else, you can take this as confirmation that the cosmic Light that enlightens every human being chooses some very strange methods of communication! The concert was by the ageing but still powerful folk group Fairport Convention, and on this particular occasion they were joined by Dave Swarbrick, making a rare appearance with his erstwhile colleagues. Swarb sang "Rosie", which is one of his signature songs, and full of resonances from my youth. Suddenly it was full of different resonances. There is no substitute for hearing it, but the words are printed just after the title page. Turn and have a quick read, and then I'll take you through the way in which my mind worked.

I was first struck by the refrain which I have quoted already: "For the more I learn, it's the less I seem to know". That seemed to me to sum up the way in which opening our eyes to complexity raises huge questions in the very areas where we used to take things for granted. Broadening our vision and awareness challenges all the old comfortable assumptions that we know where we stand and what we are doing. It must have been rather like that for Jesus' followers: the more they learned from him and worked out about him, the more they found that previous assumptions were challenged, and what they had thought was knowledge actually wasn't knowledge at all.

So that was the start. And then it came to me that much of the song could be taken as a message to the Christian churches at the start of the third millennium. I bet nothing was further from Swarb's thoughts as he wrote it, mind you, but it's funny how things work. As the first verse suggests, we are living in a very changed world. No longer do we live within the boundaries of Christendom, with our goals and our understanding of the world fashioned by the faith we have inherited. Now we live among others, and others live among us; and for some of us the old assumptions have vanished, as we have learned to live in friendship and dialogue with those around us. In the second verse we are challenged to "throw away our uniform" – for Christians, that is, to abandon the militant attitude to other faiths which we examined in chapter two, and perhaps to care a bit less about labels and badges and putting people into clearly defined categories. Certainly to care a bit less about claiming to be right. Instead, "take life by the hand" – concentrate on the humanity which we share. Concentrate on the fact that we are all faced with the dilemma of living together in the world we share, and responding properly to what is most real about this world. Concentrate on moving forward together in this world and learning from each other. Where we find that we share visions and insights, let's move forward together in harmony; where we find there is disagreement, let's not rush into argument but instead "learn to take things slow". Let's not condemn each other for being wrong, but try to work out why it is that each of us thinks we are right, and then at least we shall understand each other better.

I could build on this further, but – like the elephant – enough is enough. You can't force every detail of the song to fit my views, and I have paid my tribute now to this element of my inspiration. So where does this leave us? First of all, it leaves it absolutely clear where I stand. I have tried to take you through the process of thought and some of the experience which has led me to this point. I believe we should accept that all our religious insights and doctrines, without exception, are provisional. They are ways of trying to make sense, in human terms, of that which is far greater than us. They are the product of the human mind, the human intellect, the human emotions, trying to respond to that which makes the mind boggle and the emotions race. They are of huge value; but they are provisional. And the same applies to the insights and doctrines of other religious systems. They should be regarded as having exactly the same provisional status.

So the headline which sums up my position is, I suppose, "None of us is completely right, and all of us may be wrong". This recognizes that any claim to be right implies the unspoken but inescapable flipside that others are wrong. Yet we have no right to make that judgment so rigidly. On the other hand, to admit that we may be wrong is to admit that we still have things to learn, and that others may help us learn them. If we can get away from all the "We are right" scenarios, and admit that we are all on a level and that we are all humans groping after the truth of what is more than human, then there is some hope of us talking and thinking and learning together. Even more, there is hope of our working together to stop religious and sectarian conflict, and to bring some more harmony into the discordant relationships between religions on this troubled planet.

This does not mean abandoning our allegiance to our own religion at all, nor does it mean abandoning our zeal and our commitment to it, any more than a person should cease being devoted to a beloved partner, just because other people are devoted to other partners! Our chosen partner may be the right one for us, the one who brings out the best in us, the one whom we love; yet we will probably not regard them as perfect! In the same way the faith in which we are rooted and grounded may be the right one for us, and bring out the best in us, and we can love it warts and all. We must just recognize that one of those warts is a wart that it shares with all other religious traditions – that it is provisional and incomplete. Other religious systems may be free of some of the warts that ours has, but have different warts of their own. If we all acknowledge that this is the case, then we can remain committed to our own roots but move forward together. We can then be committed to the shared enterprise of working towards a wider vision. We can cherish our own tradition but admit that it is provisional; and on the same basis we can allow others to cherish theirs.

I started the first chapter with the statue that sits above my desk and has watched over the production of this work. It has been a symbol of many things in its time. For those who fashioned it and honored it, it was a symbol of faithfulness to tradition and respect for the ancestors who handed on their way of life from generation to generation. For the convert who parted with it to the missionary, it was a symbol of new life as a Christian and of a new service taken on without looking back. For my great-grandfather, it was a symbol of a job well done. For me, it increasingly became a symbol of an unspoken question: what exactly should the relationship be between my faith and that of other religious traditions? It is now a reminder of the process that has brought me from the Bible class to the position I hold now, which I believe is still faithful to the teaching and the person of Jesus, but involves a great change in my attitudes to the traditions of both Christianity and other religions. I would now honor certain aspects of that ancestor-cult as a response to an awareness of God, and I suppose that since I keep the statue there, I am in some fashion doing exactly that. Above all, I keep it there as a reminder of how things can change over time, in a religious tradition and in a human life. It is never too late for us to learn more, about ourselves and each other. The more we learn, the less we will seem to know, and the more we will be prepared to accept that all our understandings are provisional. The more we are prepared to accept that, the less we shall fight, and the more we shall talk, think, and work together in harmony.

Appendix one

– as promised in chapter nine...

The Blind Men of Indostan by John Godfrey Saxe

It was six men of Indostan, to learning much inclined,
Who went to see the Elephant (though all of them were blind),
That each by observation might satisfy his mind.

The *First* approach'd the Elephant, and happening to fall
Against his broad and sturdy side, at once began to bawl:
"God bless me! but the Elephant is very like a wall!"

The *Second*, feeling of the tusk, cried, "Ho! what have we here
So very round and smooth and sharp? To me 'tis mighty clear,
This wonder of an Elephant is very like a spear!"

The *Third* approach'd the animal, and happening to take
The squirming trunk within his hands, thus boldly up and spake:
"I see," – quoth he – "the Elephant is very like a snake!"

The *Fourth* reached out an eager hand, and felt about the knee:
"What most this wondrous beast is like is mighty plain" quoth he,-
"'Tis clear enough the Elephant is very like a tree!"

The *Fifth*, who chanced to touch the ear, said "E'en the blindest man
Can tell what this resembles most; deny the fact who can,
This marvel of an Elephant is very like a fan!"

The *Sixth* no sooner had begun about the beast to grope,
Then, seizing on the swinging tail that fell within his scope,
"I see," – quoth he, – "the Elephant is very like a rope!"

And so these men of Indostan disputed loud and long,
Each in his own opinion exceeding stiff and strong,
Though each was partly in the right, and all were in the wrong!

MORAL,

So, oft in theologic wars , the disputants, I ween,
Rail on in utter ignorance of what each other mean;
And prate about an Elephant not one of them has seen!

Appendix two

Further reading

There is a raft of books you could read to help you think further. What I have aimed to do here is to give a number of books which I have found it helpful to read, and which have helped to shape the thinking which lies behind this book. I have given a few remarks about each to help you decide which direction to go in; if I haven't read a book, of course I can't do that, so you won't find that this is anything like complete. But most of the books you go on to read will have bibliographies and reading lists of their own, so you'll never be short of further ideas.... I've also tried to list every book to which I have referred in the text, so you can check up on those too.

First some general suggestions for following through the issue of how different faiths should relate to each other.

For an in-depth read covering a lot of ground, you can't do better than *Andrew Wingate, Celebrating Difference, Staying Faithful, Darton, Longman & Todd, London, 2005.* The setting is British, the style scholarly but down-to-earth, and the book is founded on wide experience in both India and Britain. A similarly wide-ranging, wise, and generous book founded on a lifetime of experience and study is *Kenneth Cracknell, In Good and Generous Faith, Epworth, Peterborough, 2005.*

If you prefer easier reading – a bit easier even than mine, to be honest! – and a US background, you'll get a lot out of *M Thomas Thangaraj, Relating to People of Other Religions, Abingdon Press, Nashville, 1997.* He begins by going through the different options in something like the way I did too; but the books develop in different ways. I'll leave you to work out the differences.

And if you want a challenging overview, based on wide experience and rigorous thinking, have a go at *Martin Forward, Inter-religious Dialogue, A Short Introduction, Oneworld, Oxford, 2001.*

There are also excellent, fair explanations of exclusivism, inclusivism, and pluralism, with a lot more scholarly background, in the book which started off my academic interest in the subject: *Alan Race, Christians and Religious Pluralism, SCM, London, 2nd edition, 1993.*

For a strong representation of the exclusivist point of view (Chapter Two), try *Michael Green, "But Don't All Religions Lead To God?", Baker Books, Grand Rapids, 2002.* Green of course says they don't, and provides a clearly explained traditional view with an evangelistic message. For a more popular version of the 'because the Bible says so' approach, try the example I quoted: *Roger Carswell, Questions and Answers from the Bible, Ambassador, Belfast and Greenville, 1996.* If you want something more scholarly altogether, which adopts an exclusivist view after a robust examination of inclusivism and pluralism, try *Daniel B Clendenin, Many Gods, Many Lords, Baker Books, Grand Rapids, 1995.*

If you want to follow up the inclusivist point of view, as discussed in Chapter 4, and get to grips with Karl Rahner himself, try the 1964 address "Christianity and the Non-Christian Religions", in which he develops the idea of the "anonymous Christian". You'll find it in *Karl Rahner, Theological Investigations, Darton, Longman & Todd, London, 1966.*

For a really stimulating, if rather densely written, attempt to argue to inclusivism from a conservative evangelical background, try *Clark H Pinnock, A Wideness in God's Mercy, Zondervan, Grand Rapids, 1992.*

If you want to learn more about the theology of Justin the Martyr and the world in which it was developed, try *Henry Chadwick, The Early Church (Revised edition), Penguin, Harmondsworth, 1993* and *Von Campenhausen, The Fathers of the Greek Church, A & C Black, 1963*

And of course for the fiction of CS Lewis with which I started the chapter, take a look at *C S Lewis, The Last Battle, HarperCollins, 2005*

For pluralism (Chapter 5), well, there's a load of useful stuff. You could do worse than start with the one I quoted a lot: *John Hick, The Rainbow of Faiths, SCM, London, 1995.*

Older books of Hick's, developing the idea of the "Copernican Revolution" are *John Hick, God and the Universe of Faiths (2ⁿᵈ edition), Oneworld, Oxford, 1993,* and *John Hick, God has Many Names, Macmillan, London, 1980.*

Much is also explained in *John Hick, An Autobiography, Oneworld, Oxford, 2005.*

For Paul Knitter, try *Paul F Knitter, No Other Name?, Orbis Books, Maryknoll, 1985;* and there is a good paper by Knitter, along with much other thought-provoking stuff, in *John Hick & Paul F Knitter (eds), The Myth of Christian Uniqueness, SCM, London 1987.* Perspectives from other faiths as well as Christianity are represented well in *Paul F Knitter (ed), The Myth of Religious Superiority, Orbis, Maryknoll, 2005.*

You can't get hold of Priestland's Progress these days by the way, it's not in print, but if you really want a look, there is always Amazon

Marketplace... The details are *Gerald Priestland, Priestland's Progress, BBC, London, 1981*

Again, there is no shortage of material to follow up on the atheism debate raised in Chapter 6. The obvious starting-point at the moment is *Richard Dawkins, The God Delusion, Bantam, London, 2006*, which argues strongly against religion and against theism. Responses to such arguments include *Alister McGrath, with Joanna Collicutt McGrath, The Dawkins Delusion, SPCK London 2007*; and *Keith Ward, Is Religion Dangerous?, Lion, Oxford, 2006*; and a fuller (though earlier) survey and commentary on Dawkins' position can be found in *Alister McGrath, Dawkins' God, Blackwell, Oxford & Malden, 2005*.

Recent books by eminent scientists who demonstrate that their faith is reasoned and compatible with their science include *Francis S Collins, The Language of God, Free Press, New York, 2006* and *Owen Gingerich, God's Universe, Harvard University Press, Cambridge, 2006*

Finally, if you want to follow up on the complexity of the whole concept of God, and get a grip on many different ways in which philosophers and theologians have talked about God, you ought to have a look at *Peter Vardy and Julie Arliss, The Thinker's Guide to God, John Hunt Publishing, Alresford, 2003*. If you only look at one book from this whole list, it ought to be this one.

On Chapter 7, a good place to start on religions would be *Martin Forward, Religion, a Beginner's Guide, Oneworld, Oxford, 2001*.

For the development of doctrine, look at *Maurice F Wiles, The Making of Christian Doctrine (new edition), CUP Cambridge, 1975*, and *Maurice F Wiles, The Re-making of Christian Doctrine, SCM London, 1975* and on from there to *Maurice F Wiles, Christian Theology and Inter-Religious Dialogue, SCM London and Trinity Philadelphia, 1992*.

You might also want to pick up ideas from the discussion in *Wilfred Cantwell Smith, The Meaning and End of Religion, SPCK, London, 1978* and *Rudolf Otto, The Idea of the Holy, (English translation) Oxford University Press, London, 1923*

And on Scripture, go for *Keith Ward, What the Bible Really Teaches, SPCK, London, 2004*

And finally, if you feel like a bit of light relief and some good folk music, you'll find 'Rosie' on
Fairport Convention, Rosie, Island Masters, IMCD 152

And there is a great live version on *Swarbaid, Dave Swarbrick with Fairport Convention, live at Birmingham Symphony Hall, 6ᵗʰ March 1999, Woodworm Records WRCD032*

If that makes you want to hear more, you might try:
Fairport Convention, The Woodworm Years, Woodworm Records WRCD015, 1991; Fairport Acoustic Convention, Old, New, Borrowed and Blue, Woodworm Records WRCD024 1996; Fairport Convention, Red & Gold, HTD Records HTDCD47 1995
Fairport Convention, Shines Like Gold, Eureka Music Ltd EURCD406 1999

Or have a look at the discography on www.fairportconvention.com

Swarb himself, following major surgery, is now playing with 'Swarb's Lazarus', whose live album 'Alive and Kicking' is available from Squiggle Records. For more details take a look at www.folkicons.co.uk/swarb.htm

Whether it's theology or folk music – enjoy!

Other O-books of interest

The Bhagavad Gita

ALAN JACOBS

Alan Jacobs has succeeded in revitalising the ancient text of the Bhagavad Gita into a form which reveals the full majesty of this magnificent Hindu scripture, as well as its practical message for today's seekers. His incisive philosophic commentary dusts off all the archaism of 1500 years and restores the text as a transforming instrument pointing the way to Self Realization. – **Cygnus Review.**

9781903816516/1903816513•320pp £12.99 $19.95

Everyday Buddha

A contemporary rendering of the Buddhist classic, the Dhammapada

KARMA YONTEN SENGE (LAWRENCE ELLYARD)

Foreword by His Holiness the 14th Dalai Lama

Excellent. Whether you already have a copy of the Dhammapada or not, I recommend you get this. I congratulate all involved in this project and have put the book on my recommended list. – **Jeremy Ball**, *Nova Magazine*

9781905047307/1905047304•144pp £9.99 $19.95

Good As New

A radical retelling of the scriptures

2nd printing in hardback

A short review cannot begin to persuade readers of the value of this book. Buy it and read it. But only if you are brave enough. – **Renew**

An immensely valuable addition to scriptural understanding and appreciation. – **Methodist Recorder**

9781903816738/1903816734•448pp £19.99 $24.95 cl.
9781905047116/1905047118•448pp £11.99 $19.95 pb.

The Ocean of Wisdom

The most comprehensive compendium of worldly and spiritual wisdom this century

ALAN JACOBS

This anthology of 5,000 passages of spiritual wisdom is an awesome collection of prose and poetry, offering profound truths to everyday guidance. A valuable reference for any writer or historian, but it also makes for a good fireside or bedside book. – **Academy of Religion and Psychical Research**

9781905047079/190504707X•744pp•230x153mm £17.99 $29.95

Popol Vuh: The Sacred Book of the Maya

The Mayan creation story

ALLEN J. CHRISTENSON

The most accurate and comprehensive translation ever produced. His work is an extraordinary masterpiece of scholarly analysis. – **Karen Bassie-Sweet**, University of Calgary.

Clear, vital and entrancingly true...a brilliant exegesis, worthy of the treasure it unpacks. – **David Freidel**, Southern Methodist University

9781903816530/190381653X•320pp•230x153mm £19.95 $29.95

Popol Vuh II

A literal, line by line translation

ALLEN J. CHRISTENSON

A definitive document of rhetorical brilliance. – **Stephen Houston**, Jesse Knight University Professor, Brigham Young University

An invaluable contribution... **Justin Kerr**, author of *The Maya Vase books*.

9781903816578/1903816572•280pp•230x153mm £25.00 $37.50

The Principal Upanishads

ALAN JACOBS

Alan Jacobs has produced yet another literary masterpiece in his transcreation of the 'Principal Upanishads', which together with his 'Bhagavad Gita', aim to convey the nondualist teaching (Advaita Vedanta) of the ancient Indian scriptures as well as explore the author's own poetic expression. – **Paula Marvelly**

9781903816509/1903816505•384pp £12.99 $19.95

The Spiritual Wisdom of Marcus Aurelius
Practical philosophy from an ancient master
ALAN JACOBS

Most translations are literal and arid but Jacobs has paraphrased a selection of the best of Aurelius' meditations so as to give more force to the essential truths of his philosophy. – **The Light**

There's an uncanny appropriateness of this work to current times so this book is bound to resonate with many. – **Wave**

9781903816745/1903816742•260pp £9.99 $14.95

A World Religions Bible
ROBERT VAN DE WEYER

An admirable book to own personally for reflection and meditation, with the possibility of contemplating a different extract a day over an entire year. It is our hope that the use of this splendid anthology will grow. We recommend it to all for their personal enrichment. – **The Friend**

Outstanding collection of religious wisdom...never has so much wisdom been concentrated in such a small space. – **New Age Retailer**

9781903816158/1903816157•432pp•full colour•180x120mm £19.99 $28.95

A Heart for the World
The interfaith alternative
MARCUS BRAYBROOKE

This book is really needed. This is the blueprint. It has to be cherished. Faith in Jesus is not about creeds or homilies. It is a willingness to imitate Christ-as the Hindu guru Gandhi did so well. A must book to buy. – **Peacelinks**, IFOR

9781905047437/1905047436•168pp £12.99 $24.95

Bringing God Back to Earth
JOHN HUNT

Knowledgeable in theology, philosophy, science and history. Time and again it is remarkable how he brings the important issues into relation with one another... thought provoking in almost every sentence, difficult to put down. – **Faith and Freedom**

Absorbing, highly readable, profound and wide ranging. – **The Unitarian**

9781903816813/1903816815•320pp £9.99 $14.95

Christ Across the Ganges
Hindu responses to Jesus
SANDY BHARAT

This is a fascinating and wide-ranging overview of a subject of great importance. It is a must for anyone interested in the history of religious traditions and in the interaction between faiths. – **Marianne Rankin**, Alister Hardy Society

9781846940002/1846940001•224pp•230x153mm £14.99 $29.95

A Global Guide to Interfaith
Reflections from around the world
SANDY AND JAEL BHARAT

For those who are new to interfaith this amazing book will give a wonderful picture of the variety and excitement of this journey of discovery. It tells us something about the world religions, about interfaith history and organizations, how to plan an interfaith meeting and much more – mostly through the words of practitioners. – **Marcus Braybrooke**

9781905047970/1905047975•336pp•230x153mm £19.99 $34.95

The Hindu Christ
Jesus' message through Eastern eyes
JOHN MARTIN SAHAJANANDA

To the conventional theologian steeped in the Judaeo-Christian tradition, this book is challenging and may even be shocking at times. For mature Christians and thinkers from other faiths, it makes its contribution to an emerging Christian theology from the East that brings in a new perspective to Christian thought and vision. – **Westminster Interfaith**

9781905047550/190504755X•128pp £9.99 $19.95

The History of Now
A guide to higher yearnings
ANDY NATHAN

This is all about the spark of optimism that gets us out of bed in the morning, and the different ways it has flared to life during the time of humanity. A "who's who" of the world religions.

9781903816288/1903816289•160pp•250x153mm £9.99

Islam and the West

Inside the mind of God

ROBERT VAN DE WEYER

2nd printing

Argues that though in the sphere of economics and politics relationships between Islam and the West have often been hostile, in the area of ideas and philosophy the two have much in common, indeed are interdependent. A military and financial jihad against global terrorism cannot be won. Bit a jihad for peace can, and will render the first jihad unnecessary.

9781903816141/1903816149•128pp £6.99

Trading Faith

Global religion in an age of rapid change

DAVID HART

Argues boldly that the metaphor of trading provides the most useful model for religious exchanges in a world of rapid change. It is the inspiring biography of an intensely spiritual man with a great sense of humour who has chosen an unusual and courageous religious path. – **Dr Anna King**, Lecturer in Hinduism, University of Winchester

9781905047963/1905047967•260pp £10.99 $24.95

Transcending Terror

A history of our spiritual quest and the challenge of the new millennium

IAN HACKETT

Looks at the history of the major world religions, paying particular to nine great prophets, their teachings and what later generations have made of them. All are presented as stemming from the human quest for truth in every age. – **Westminster Interfaith**

9781903816875/1903816874•320pp £12.99 $19.95

You Are the Light

Rediscovering the Eastern Jesus

JOHN MARTIN SHAJANANDA

2nd printing

Closed systems, structures and beliefs have prevailed over the last 2000 years, cutting off the majority from direct contact with God and sharing Jesus's own insight on non-duality. This is an inspiring new contemplative vision. – **Scientific and Medical Network Review**

9781903816301/1903816300•224pp £9.99 $15.95

The Barefoot Indian

The making of a messiahress

JULIA HEYWOOD

Spiritual fiction, or not? Eternal wisdom is expressed in the context of modern day to day life, in a fresh, sensitive, intuitive, humorous and profoundly inspirational way.

9781846940408/1846940400•196pp £9.99 $19.95

The Soulbane Illusion

NORMAN JETMUNDSEN

Truly great writing…I was inspired. It is something I can recommend to anyone interested in the supernatural/thriller with a foundational faith to inspire people. If you like the works of C S Lewis, you will like this; if you like the works of John Grisham, you will like this. A good blend of the two. – **Roundtable Review**

9781903816592/1903816599•308pp £7.99 $12.95

The Soulbane Stratagem

NORMAN JETMUNDSEN

2nd printing

Listed by Wesley Owen as one of the all-time top 10 great Christian fiction titles. *Rewarding, perhaps even life-changing; a readable, spiritually instructive work which should find a wide market.* – **The Anniston Star**

An engaging style of writing, an engrossing tale…truly exhilarating, a significant contribution to modern day theology. – **Birmingham Bar**

9781903019696/1903019699•296pp £6.99 $12.95

Souls Don't Lie

A true story of past lives

JENNY SMEDLEY

People often go on about past lives they believe they've had, but rarely has anyone explained so eloquently and succinctly the art and science of using past-life regression to heal the life you're living now – a fascinating and recommended read. – **Barefoot Doctor**, healer and author.

9781905047833/1905047835•224pp £11.99 $19.95

Head Versus Heart-and our Gut Reactions

The 21st century enneagram

MICHAEL HAMPSON

A seminal work, whose impact will continue to reverberate throughout the 21st century. Brings illumination and allows insights to tumble out. – **Fr Alexander**, Worth Abbey

9781903816929/19038169020•320pp £11.99 $16.95

The Quest

Exploring a sense of soul

DAWES, DOLLEY AND ISAKSEN

This remarkable course draws on a wide variety of psychospiritual approaches. Not another hyped up DIY book but rather a carefully considered and comprehensive guide. Invaluable. – **Scientific and Medical Network Review**

9781903816936/1903816939•264pp £9.99 $16.95

Zen Economics

Save the world and yourself by saving

ROBERT VAN DE WEYER

This book carries several messages of hope, which are linked by the theme of saving and investing. Its single most important message is that in the western world most of us have reached a point of prosperity where the investment with the highest rate of return is investing in the self.

9781903816783/1903816785•96pp £9.99 $14.95

O books
O is a symbol of the world, of oneness and unity. In different cultures it also means the "eye", symbolizing knowledge and insight, and in Old English it means "place of love or home". O books explores the many paths of understanding which different traditions have developed down the ages, particularly those

BOOKS

today that express respect for the planet and all of life. In philosophy, metaphysics and aesthetics O as zero relates to infinity, indivisibility and fate. In Zero Books we are developing a list of provocative shorter titles that cross different specializations and challenge conventional academic or majority opinion.

For more information on the full list of over 300 titles please visit our website
www.O-books.net